# QUIET VOICES

## Reflections of Twentieth Century Women

Written and Compiled by
## The Quiet Hour Club of Metuchen

ANYA JOHNSON/Los Angeles Times Syndicate

# QUIET VOICES

Reflections of Twentieth Century Women

Written and compiled by

## The Quiet Hour Club of Metuchen

Founded in 1895

Copyright © 2000 by The Quiet Hour Club of Metuchen.

| Library of Congress Number: | | 00-190581 |
|---|---|---|
| ISBN #: | Hardcover | 0-7388-1850-X |
| | Softcover | 0-7388-1851-8 |

All rights reserved. No part of this book may be reproduced or transmitted in any form or by any means, electronic or mechanical, including photocopying, recording, or by any information storage and retrieval system, without permission in writing from the copyright owner.

This book was printed in the United States of America.

**To order additional copies of this book, contact:**
Xlibris Corporation
1-888-7-XLIBRIS
www.Xlibris.com
Orders@Xlibris.com

# CONTENTS

FOREWORD
    Rev. Barbara C. Crafton .................................................. 9
THE QUIET HOUR CLUB OF
METUCHEN, NEW JERSEY ............................................. 11

## THE EARLY DAYS OF THE CENTURY

PARUMAL
    Elsie Potter ..................................................................... 19
CHINA OF MY CHILDHOOD
    Catherine Klingler ......................................................... 24

## THE NINETEEN TWENTIES

CHRISTMAS MEMORIES
    Dorothy Coleman ......................................................... 29
GROWING UP IN THE TWENTIES
    Emily Jolley .................................................................... 33
CAPTAIN TOLFSEN, MY GRANDPA
    Mildred Jones ................................................................ 36

## THE NINETEEN THIRTIES

CHRISTMAS FLASHBACKS
    Lorraine Bachman ......................................................... 43
MEETING THE FAMILY AT AGE TWENTY-FIVE
    Hildegard Goodenough ................................................. 46
NEW YORK SCHOOLDAYS
    Gloria Marino ................................................................ 50
BLIZZARDS AND HOBOS
    Elinor McCann .............................................................. 53

ROADS WELL TRAVELED
    VIRGINIA OKELL .................................................... 57
THE LITTLE CHURCH
    JANE PALMETER ..................................................... 61
BACKSTAGE DAUGHTER
    MARNIE SMITH ........................................................ 65
SUMMER IN THE COUNTRY
    MARIAN STONE ....................................................... 68
TRIPS ACROSS THE COUNTRY
    CAROL TOWT .......................................................... 72
MY GRANDPARENTS' GENES
    NANCY WRIGHT ...................................................... 75
SELF DISCOVERY
    ANNA YOUNG .......................................................... 78

## THE NINETEEN FORTIES

THREE
    LYNN BERGNER ....................................................... 83
MY MOTHER—SHE KNEW HOW
    JUNE DURKEE .......................................................... 86
POIGNANT RECOLLECTIONS
    JUDITH HASSERT ..................................................... 89
A WAR-TIME REMINISCENCE
WITH MY GRANDSON
    MARY JONES ........................................................... 92
A SPECIAL YEAR OF MY LIFE
    GERDA WOERNER .................................................... 95

## THE NINETEEN FIFTIES

MY LETTER TO MY
GREAT-GRANDCHILDREN-TO-BE
    Dr. Felonese Kelley .................................................... 101
A FRENCH STREET PERSPECTIVE
    Melody Kokola ............................................................ 105
DRESS REHEARSAL
    Mary Ellen Malague .................................................. 108

## THE NINETEEN SIXTIES

READ THIS WHEN YOU'RE ALL GROWN UP
    Rev. Barbara C. Crafton ............................................ 115
TYROLEAN POLENTA PARTIES
    Carol Cuneo ............................................................... 119
THE CANASTA GAME
    Bette Daniele .............................................................. 123

## THE NINETEEN SEVENTIES

EUROPE BY CAMPER
    Roberta Ambler .......................................................... 129
ON WINGS OF JOY
    Alberta Bachman ....................................................... 133
BRINGING UP PARENTS
    Ellen Donahay ........................................................... 137
PIQUE-NIQUE
    Audray Noyes ............................................................. 141

## THE NINETEEN EIGHTIES

**GOING HOME**
    Muriel Cagney .................................................................. 147

**TRANSFORMATION**
    Jessie Flynn ...................................................................... 151

**THROUGH THE LOOKING GLASS**
    Helen Stapley .................................................................. 154

## THE NINETEEN NINETIES

**NEWPORT, OREGON—1998**
    Bernice Bransfield ......................................................... 161

**A NIGHT AT THE OPERA**
    Frances Hansen .............................................................. 165

**FAMILY REUNION**
    Janet Phillips .................................................................. 167

# FOREWORD

## Rev. Barbara Cawthorne Crafton

A whole millennium is just too much responsibility. There is no adequate way to say good-bye to it, no adieu of sufficient heft to stop us all in our tracks and make us say, "Yep. That says it all." You can't say it all about a thousand years.

But then, you can't say it all about a century, either. The turn of this one into the next has precipitated—in spades—what every new year precipitates: lists of ultimates. The best this, the most that, the ten most fascinating people, the man of the century, the most arresting photograph, the number one song. These projects, too, are doomed; a century's worth of history can't be distilled to a single point. There was just too much going on.

So we chose our own lifetimes. We wrote letters to those who will survive us, tried to tell them the most important things we wanted them to know about our sojourn on the earth. But even in this, even in our own small lives, we had trouble. Lives just don't sum up very well. They don't mean just one thing. They can't fit into just one memory. They are complex skeins of moments, the quietest of them brilliant in its many strands.

And so, in the letters that follow, we have done with our lives what people have always done when they tried to tell their stories; we have told a piece of the story, captured a moment, large or small, and passed it on. We have offered a piece of our own memories to the common memory. We have not said it all. But each of us has spoken her piece.

# THE QUIET HOUR CLUB OF METUCHEN, NEW JERSEY

## 1895-2000

On the seventh day of November in 1895, Mrs. Hester M. Poole, a woman who had previously started the International Council for Women, set about on a new mission—one she later described in the club's objectives as "bringing together women in Metuchen, New Jersey, for mental culture, social interchange, and sympathetic understanding of whatever women are doing along the best line of progress." And so was founded The Quiet Hour Club of Metuchen.

Mrs. Poole was a small, dignified woman, well known as a writer, an authority on parliamentary law, and an ardent feminist of the Nineteenth Century. When nominated for the presidency of Sorosis, the famous pioneer women's club of the Nineteenth Century, she declined in order to give more time to The Quiet Hour Club.

During the early club meetings, time was devoted to reading and discussion of one person, one country, or one part of the world. Mrs. Poole enjoyed the music performed during these meetings, particularly when Mrs. Prickitt came in with her "youthful enthusiasm and supple fingers" at the piano. Her home was a mecca for distinguished friends, among them Clara Barton, Susan B. Anthony, Frances Willard, and Elizabeth Cady Stanton.

The name "The Quiet Hour Club" has puzzled outsiders for one hundred and four years. Early members intended that "the club provide time for the women to pursue their own intellectual interests away from concern of domestic life." Mrs. Poole, although a feminist, wanted to exclude from this club all talk of religion, politics, and family life, to allow time for discussions of female issues and literary pursuits. In all this time, no member has taken the title literally, however, and the discussions are generally quite lively.

From the beginning, meetings have been run quite formally, with a slate of officers, a constitution, and by-laws. Membership then and now is by nomination, and membership has been restricted to thirty members to permit the comfortable use of members' homes, where meetings are held.

The format of the meetings has changed very little in the club's lengthy history. At the first meeting, a poem by Eugene Field, a brief prose extract from one of Lowell's letters on Emerson, and a portion of Emerson's "Essay on Compensation" were read; spirited discussion followed this erudite program. Other topics of those early meetings were "New Jersey in the Time of the Revolution," "A Visit to Athens," and "The Effects of a College Education on a Woman's Ability to Manage Her Home." Records indicate that several meetings were devoted to a discussion of the women's suffrage movement, but the club did not take a stand on either the suffrage or temperance movement.

Current events were discussed at every meeting. The office of Chronicler was established specifically to guarantee that the women be kept up on global issues. Many of the women had traveled abroad, so experiences were also shared at meetings. As the years progressed, a single topic was chosen for study each year, with each member writing a paper on some aspect of that topic; currently, two such papers are read after the brief business meeting. The minutes note that in the 1920s, Mrs. Harold Edgar "gave an original paper on 'The Poet's Italy' of such unusual interest and breadth that she carried the audience away with her into a dreamy ideal atmosphere." An office that did not last through the century was the role of Critic, whose job it was to keep a running list of pronunciation errors made throughout the year and present it at the final meeting.

In the early days, despite the club's apolitical stance, it contributed to various projects in the town of Metuchen. For example, noted are the purchase of a waste paper receptacle for Main Street, the placement of an encyclopedia in the Middlesex Water Company for the use of the townspeople, the pleas for clean streets and preserved trees, a boycott of German articles following World War I, a sizeable contribution to the building of the Metuchen Library, and clear support for the establishment of New Jersey College for Women.

At the fourth meeting of the Quiet Hour Club, members voted to join the State Federation of Women's Clubs and proceeded to send delegates to meetings and conventions. There was a great spirit of solidarity among the local clubs, particularly with women's clubs in New Brunswick and Perth Amboy. However, when the other clubs chose to make priorities of fund raising and services, the Quiet Hour members chose to remain primarily a study club; and so it continues to this day.

From the very start, an open meeting has been held annually to which guests are invited to hear the members read their papers on their annual topic and, at times, to enjoy a guest speaker. As a break from the intellectual program, the final meeting of the year traditionally takes the form of a picnic. Hospitality was at a peak in the 1930s, when Mrs. Coerr arranged to have her oriental rugs brought out from her home, the site of the picnic, to protect the ladies' shoes. As a part of each meeting, the custom of preparing a delightful tea table, complete with silver service and tea pourers, becomes the pleasure of the hostess, each member taking a turn at two-year intervals. Hats and gloves were eliminated in the 1960s, but cordiality, friendliness, graciousness, and respect for tradition have become hallmarks of the meetings of The Quiet Hour of Metuchen.

As we move into the Twenty-first Century, approximately thirty women of the Metuchen area make the same commitment today as their foremothers did in 1895. Each spends weeks in reading and writing to carefully prepare her paper so that she can successfully educate and entertain the other members of the club at her appointed time. In recent years, annual topics have included "The Victorian Era," "American Presidents and Their Families," "Contemporary Women in a Changing World," "The Poet and His Verse," "The Artist and His Canvas," "Paris in the Twenties," "A Study of Early Civilizations," and "Inventors and Their Inventions."

Yes, one hundred and four years have passed, but Foundress Hester Poole and her twelve charter members could visit a Twenty-first Century meeting and feel right at home.

By Judith Hassert and Mary Ellen Malague

# THE EARLY DAYS OF THE CENTURY

# PARUMAL

## Elsie B. Potter

Dear Children,

    I found the enclosed in one of the boxes I hadn't opened since moving to Maine. "Bam," your grandmother, wrote it many years ago and subsequently presented it as a paper for the Quiet Hour Club.

\* \* \* \* \* \* \* \*

For two and a half unforgettable years, I lived in South India. I was a young woman at the time and keenly alive to new experiences. Out of all the rich treasures of those experiences, I prize most my friendship with Parumal, a servant.

    Parumal was dark-skinned and his wrinkled, leathery face gave little clue to his age. On rare occasions when he talked of himself, he told of serving master after master, vaguely indicating many, many years of service. But this unlettered Indian knew little of the facts of arithmetic, so his age is simply conjecture.

    From 1913 to 1918, my husband was principal of Voorhees College, a mission school in Vellore, India, and it was he who first encountered Parumal, the faithful servant of many an inexperienced westerner. Parumal, in fact, was a legacy which went with the office of principal, to which my husband had succeeded. My turn to meet Parumal was to come later.

    Although deeply loyal to each previous master, Parumal gave the same untiring, unselfish devotion to each new one. So he soon became the trusted ally of Dr. Potter, a lonely young bachelor trying to accommodate himself to the conditions of a new and strange land.

A year and one half later in 1914, my future husband made a quick trip back to America, leaving Parumal in a daze of uncertainty as to why "Master" should risk a wartime voyage. However, all this was soon revealed. In the course of a two-month stay at home, "Master" became engaged and married.

Following our marriage in 1915, my husband and I began the long ten-week trek by ship across the Pacific to get back to India.

What a wonderful reception awaited me in my Indian home! Everyone received us with the sympathy and friendliness which characterizes the Indian. But nowhere was there quite so much joy as in our own household with Parumal beaming a welcome to young "Missy," as he immediately named me. The two following years in our old Indian bungalow were an idyll over which Parumal presided.

Parumal's training over the years must have been remarkable, for he was both cook and butler combined. He prepared all sorts of exotic dishes in a little shack located a hundred paces from our bungalow door. He served up the hot food himself with great flair, and nothing ever daunted him. If I appeared just before dinner with one or more unexpected guests and anxiously consulted him as to the possibilities of entertainment, he would assume a grave expression and invariably reply, "I'll manage." And manage he would. The soup might be thinner and the portions of the following courses rather minute, but he never let "young Missy" down.

Parumal watched over us both with the loving care of a mother. He darned our stockings, packed our bags, laid out our clothes, polished our shoes, and saw to it that each day "Missy" had a fresh homemade corsage lying on the dresser when she came out of her bath. He also went to the bazaar to make the daily purchases and would return each noon with a long memorandum known to Indian households as the "account book." Another duty involved hiring the other servants and arranging about their pay, whether they were five or six rupees a month, and keeping careful watch as to their efforts, promptly dismissing them if they did not measure up to expectations.

There was nothing that our "guardian" could or would not do. If either of us was sick, no one could have been kinder or more concerned, and his dear old face would light up with joy when "Master" or "Missy" was well again.

We were young in years and the servants young in spirit, making housekeeping a delightful game. Somehow Parumal came to know what were our special days and never failed to mark them with some charming bit of ceremony. There was never any worry about forgetting anniversaries. If it was "Master's" birthday, we would find no chair at his place in the dining room. Great excitement would ensue. Where was "Master's" chair? Servant boys would run in every direction with Parumal calling orders in Tamil. Each room would be searched. Finally, from the back veranda would come a pair of grinning boys bearing between them the chair, completely covered with roses, jasmine, and palm leaves, a veritable bower of beauty. Then "Master" would be enthroned at the table.

When "Missy's" birthday or a wedding anniversary came around, the drama was enacted again. The procedure was always the same—the missing chair, the scurrying and searching, and then the discovery of the floral throne. It was a delightful drama which never palled.

In due time there was a blessed event in our little family, and enthusiasm rose to new heights. On the great day when my baby and I returned from the hospital, the whole house had been polished to greet us. On the steps to the veranda, rugs were spread end to end to give the impression of a royal welcome.

Old Parumal took the new "young Master" to his heart with, if possible, an even deeper affection than that he had shown to us. There are hazards to a young life in India, but never was an infant so shielded from them.

One night, when the anxious young father and mother mustered up sufficient courage to go out for the evening, we returned to a scene which I can never forget. It was one of those scenes which will always make India and her people dear to me. At the veranda stood the college messenger boy with bicycle at his side, ready to hurry and seek us if anything untoward should develop; a little farther on, another white-robed form arose from the floor where he had been sleeping—Parumal's brother, summoned as special guard; inside the doorway lay Parumal himself, who arose with ready salaams to assure us that all was well with the sleeping infant. And finally, at the side of the crib was the ayah, or Indian nurse, watching over the little one.

Almost the same watchfulness was extended to me on those occasions when my husband had to be away on college business over night. Then Parumal would bring a blanket and stretch his old limbs on the floor across the threshold of my door. Often he was found there faithfully and literally carrying out his instructions to take good care of me.

Unfortunately, our Indian idyll was cut short all too soon when my husband contracted malaria. Somehow, while the Indian was friendly and sympathetic, the Indian climate was less hospitable. It was a sad day for Parumal when the little family took its departure. Down the street we rode in an old fashioned buggy drawn by the willing hands of a crowd of Indian students. Behind in a humbler conveyance went Parumal, with several steamer trunks and boxes of belongings.

On the following morning we arrived at the station in Madras and boarded the train for Columbo, where we would embark on the long sea voyage home over the Pacific. As we sat in our compartment awaiting the departure of the train, Parumal stood on the platform outside while I held the baby at the open window. There our dear friend stood with tears streaming down his face as he held one of the child's bare feet in his hand and rubbed it up and down his face. "What will Parumal do without young master?" he asked. But with the Hindu's idea of rebirth, he talked of young master's return to India someday as a young man. Then Parumal would be a little "Chokra" boy again and would serve him.

God bless him and his dear, faithful heart. Did I call him a "servant"? He was more than that. He was my friend—a caring, strong support to a young woman making her home in a strange land. If I can ever show a tithe of his faithfulness and be rewarded in heaven, I'm sure I will find him waiting for me with a special cup of nectar, and he will find a royal carpet to lay on the celestial steps to greet "young Missy."

* * * * * * * *

> Much love,
> Mom
> (June Potter Durkee)

*Elsie B. Potter (d. 1980) lived all her life in Metuchen, with the exception of a period in India when she was first married. She raised three children, was an avid reader, quoting Shakespeare, Longfellow, and Dickens at length, and was a delight to her children and grandchildren.*

# CHINA OF MY CHILDHOOD

## Catherine Klingler

Dear Sarah Beth,

How honored I am that you want to know more about my years in China! I was born in Canton, China, on October 28, 1911, just after the Manchus were overthrown by Sun Yat-sen and his followers. My father, a teacher and school administrator, and my mother, a nurse, had responded to a call by the Student Volunteer Movement for Foreign Missions and met in Canton.

Its beginnings were humble. Property was bought on Honam Island. It was a very irregular-shaped piece of land of about 30 acres, with narrow access to the river along a canal, and consisting mostly of former rice fields between the hills, which were covered with graves. There were several temporary wooden buildings, a single brick bungalow, and Martin Hall, a building used for classrooms, library, offices, labs, and residences. (I was born in one of the rooms on the top floor—now a library storeroom.) From only a middle school for 35 boys, the school grew to include girls, facilities for children of foreign staff, dormitories, and faculty residences. It educated people from kindergarten through graduate school. Before the Japanese occupation, there were over 2,000 students on a campus of 450 acres.

Even though I was born in the last days of the Ching Dynasty, lived through the early pangs of the Republic as well as anti-foreign and labor troubles, crossed the Pacific during WW I, where

German submarines were on the prowl, and lived in Shanghai at boarding school when the Generalissimo won out over the Communist faction, I have memories of a happy childhood. It is truly a blessing to have the best of two cultures influencing one's life. How wonderful to never have to think whether or not we were with a Chinese or American or worry about when to speak Chinese or English!

Of course, I have to admit it was an insulated life. We lived in a beautiful home, surrounded by loving and caring people—especially the amah whose only English was "Hey, hi, naughty girl"—amidst a beautiful tropical landscape that included tennis courts, concrete walks on which to roller skate or ride bikes, and a pony to ride (a delight in spite of occasional falls into smelly paddy fields). I remember we had short hair cuts because Father said it was too hot to have long hair. And never mind the styles! We did have to wear pith hats (On Sundays fancy doilies were put on them.), and that was a nuisance. And we were very healthy, eating lots of fresh fruits and vegetables, all grown on the college farm.

Every five years we came to the United States for a sabbatical. Father studied and did research on nutrition and conducted a lot of university business. Mother kept house, cooked (although it was not her favorite occupation), and spoke at missionary society meetings where my sister and I were exhibited in Chinese clothes and sang "Jesus Loves Me" in Chinese. She nursed us through all the childhood diseases we had missed in China. On the whole, the family enjoyed the change, and my sisters and I knew it was good for us to learn more about America. But we were always glad when it was time to go home . . . to China. I realized soon how fortunate we were to live in China and felt more at home there than in America.

Nevertheless, following boarding school in Shanghai, I entered Pomona College in Claremont, California. After graduating in 1932, I attended Columbia University School of Library Service and then happily went "home" to work at the college library. I finally decided that I was an American and belonged in the USA, so I came back to work as Librarian of the East Asiatic Collections at Columbia University. In 1941, my parents were forced into a Japanese internment camp in Hong Kong, and I felt impelled to join the WAVES to express my concern for them and my support for the United States. In 1950, all foreigners left China, and our beloved college became a government university.

No doubt, you will understand when I say that, although I married and lived happily here in New Jersey throughout my adult life, the China of my youth has formed much of who I am and will remain a sweet memory in my heart.

Love,<br>Nanny

*Catherine Klingler spent an idyllic childhood in her birthplace, China. After attending Pomona College and Columbia University School of Library Service, she oversaw the East Asiatic Collection at Columbia and later, Rutgers University Libraries. Following World War II service in the WAVES, Katie settled in a restored eighteenth century Dutch Colonial, where she married and raised two children. She is currently residing in Louisville, Kentucky.*

# THE NINETEEN TWENTIES

# CHRISTMAS MEMORIES

## Dorothy Coleman

Dear Rebecca,

It was such a pleasure to receive your letter telling me of the wonderful Christmas you spent with your baby daughter and handsome little son, my great-grandchildren. Having great-grandchildren has made me realize I am indeed an elderly lady. Yet I can remember a Christmas when I was five years old that, in my memory, seems to have occurred just a few years ago.

My grandparents came to our house on Christmas Eve for dinner. Dinner wasn't served until six o'clock, since this was a busy time of year for my Grandfather Shannon, who was a florist. Our tree was already set up in the sun porch. But it was not trimmed, for Santa Claus would do that after we had gone to bed.

After dinner I would receive presents from my grandparents, and then it would be time to hang up my stocking. This was hung on a mantelpiece that contained an opening for a radiant heater but not a real fire. I became more and more excited and kept putting my head into the opening of the fireplace and saying, "I think I hear him now." Therefore, I was anxious to go to bed so Santa would have plenty of time to lay out my presents and trim the tree.

After many warnings from my parents not to stay awake or Santa would not come, I went upstairs. In my arms was my favorite companion, a Puss-in-Boots made of red and blue oil cloth. I'm afraid my grandchildren would not have thought he was very attractive.

During the night I awakened, and I could feel Santa Claus's arm resting on my legs as he leaned over to make sure I was asleep. I did not move, and I hardly breathed. I was so afraid he wouldn't leave my gifts.

When morning came, I opened my eyes very slowly; it was daylight and poor Puss-in-Boots lay across my legs. It hadn't been Santa after all. I gave Puss a big hug.

By now my father had the coal furnace going and had turned on the radiant heater. The tree was lit, my stocking was filled, and many presents were under the tree.

By the time I was nine, although I did not believe in Santa Claus anymore, I had no problem adjusting. My grandparents still came on Christmas Eve, and the tree still stood in the sunporch. But now we trimmed it the day before.

That Christmas I was told that my father was making me a dollhouse, my very favorite toy. Others I had were small. He was making the house in the basement, and it was covered with a sheet. I was warned not to peek under the sheet, and I did not do that, for I love surprises.

In those days one was able to get a large orange crate from a grocer. My father nailed two of them together lengthwise, one on top of the other. So my house had four large rooms. There was carpeting on the floor, and curtains hung at the window openings. What really excited me was a lamp that was lit in the living room. The battery was hidden behind the baby grand piano. There was a fireplace with crinkled red paper for the fire and, for my baby doll, a white bassinet with white net drifting over the sides. Oh, I loved that dollhouse as I have loved my different homes as an adult. Even in my present little apartment, I have a little antique-looking wooden medicine chest that has been converted into a dollhouse with a plain glass door so guests can see the three shelves I have finished. The bottom shelf is a kitchen; the middle shelf, a living room; and the top shelf, a nursery. Friends contribute small things such as a miniature book, a wall telephone, and a Christmas tree for the holidays.

When I got married, Christmas was still exciting. We would go to my mother's for Christmas dinner but open our presents to each other at home. Being an only child, I had received many presents in those days, so I said to my husband, "If you have just ten dollars to spend, I'd rather have ten one-dollar gifts than one ten-dollar gift." After many years of marriage, he was fond of telling people, "And I'm still giving her ten one-dollar gifts." It was just a joke. I remember one year my mother asked my husband what he was going to give me, and he answered, "An Elgin watch." She exclaimed that that was a lovely present, and she told me that he answered, "But she's worth it!" Though the watch doesn't work anymore, I still have it. I also have a red plaid Pendleton suit he bought, and I am still wearing it even though it is now thirty years old and the hem has been raised and lowered many times.

When our daughter reached two years of age, we set up a small tree in her room, and I slept on a cot next to her crib to watch her first reaction to the lit tree. But to my disappointment, she never noticed it. But years later, she told me she had always received everything she had wanted at Christmas.

When my son was nine years old, we bought a nice new bicycle for him and hid it in a neighbor's home. After my son went to bed, my husband went to get the bicycle. As he was wheeling it around to the back door, my son opened his window and called, "Hi, Dad!" My husband wanted to throw one of the rocks in the flowerbed at him. But George has always said he couldn't see the bike in the dark.

I have been a widow for many years now, but I go to my daughter's home in Ohio for Christmas and spend Thanksgiving with my son and his family. Now I have many grandchildren and great-grandchildren, and I know how fortunate I am. Sometimes there is a fierce longing in my heart to do it all over again with my husband still there to enjoy our large family with me. But I am sure he sees us and is still putting aside ten one-dollar gifts to give me when we are together again.

Love,
Nana

*Dorothy Coleman, a native of Brooklyn, New York, and a graduate of the Berkeley Institute, is the past president of the Perth Amboy Women's Auxiliary, the women's division of the Metuchen YMCA, The Borough Improvement League of Metuchen, and the Quiet Hour Club. Presently, she serves as a volunteer with Hospice. She is the mother of two, grandmother of eight, and great-grandmother of six.*

# GROWING UP IN THE TWENTIES

## Emily Jolley

Dear Barbara,

I decided to write about the early years. One of the best periods of my life was as a child growing up in the 1920s, after World War I and before the Great Depression. It was a peaceful, happy time for me.

I lived in a seven room house on a half acre of property in Highland Park, NJ, with my parents, brother, and sister. We had a big front porch and spent many hours there with family and friends. My father had built the house, and we had all the modern conveniences—running water, inside bathroom, and electricity. Because electricity was fairly new, my father had gas jets installed so we would have light if the electricity failed. We had a washing machine with a wringer in a laundry room in the basement. There was a cement floor in the basement, and in bad weather we played there, even roller skated.

We had many friends, but the best times were as a family. My father had a big leather chair where he usually sat in the living room. He would sit there and read the paper when he came home from work. When he put the paper down, the three of us piled on the chair with him until dinner was ready. Sometimes he read to us, sometimes he told us stories, and sometimes we just talked.

After dinner, when everything was cleared up and put away, the three of us sat around the dining room table, and my mother would read the comics to us. Then we played board games or simple card games until bedtime, which was nine o'clock most nights.

My mother was very fond of music, and we had a victrola, the kind you wind up and hope it doesn't run down before the record is finished playing. We would all sit in the living room and enjoy the music. When radio was new, my father bought one, and we would spend some evenings listening to programs that he chose.

My father had two sisters who lived in New Brunswick, and we spent every Sunday and holiday with them. They came to our house one week, and we went there the next. The trip to New Brunswick was by trolley, and the fare was five cents.

There weren't any electric refrigerators in the homes then. Everyone had an icebox, and the ice man came all summer. We had a card to put in the front window to let him know how big a piece we wanted—25 pounds, 50 pounds, or 100 pounds. While he was taking the ice around to the kitchen, the children, including us, would climb in the back of the truck and "steal" a piece of ice. I am sure he knew we would because there were always small chunks near the back of the truck, and we were all out front, sucking on ice when he got back to the truck.

There weren't any super markets then. When we went shopping, we went to several stores and more than once a week. We shopped at a grocery store, a butcher shop, vegetable market, bakery, and a drug store. Most drug stores had a soda fountain, and this was where my father went every Saturday night for ice cream for us. We also had a candy store where we could get wonderful things for a penny. We knew all the shopkeepers by name, and they knew us.

When I was about seven years old, my aunt took me to the movies. The picture was "Rin Tin Tin." He was a beautiful dog and did marvelous things, like rescuing drowning people and pulling people from burning buildings. It was a silent movie with the words people were speaking written at the lower part of the screen. There was a grand piano in the front of the theater, and a man played throughout the show. As the scenes became more exciting, the music did too.

A short time after that, a theater was built in Highland Park to project the current rage, talking pictures. On Saturday afternoons, the three of us and some of our friends would go to the movies, and we saw such exciting things as Tom Mix and Hoot Gibson saving people or towns from all sorts of problems and bad guys. We got to see a double feature, a newsreel, and a cartoon—all for ten cents. If we stayed too late, we would see one of our mothers coming down the aisle with an usher, and we'd all go home.

My grandmother lived in Belmar, and every summer we spent two weeks there. We got down to the ocean and played in the sand, and we were allowed to go barefoot. We also got to visit with aunts, uncles, and cousins there.

My mother's uncle had a farm in Wall Township that we loved to visit. He had chickens, horses, cows, and pigs, and we always looked forward to spending a day with him. There were no modern conveniences and, as "city kids," we were fascinated with the outside pump and the outhouse. We even enjoyed the smell of the kerosene stove and lamps.

I have many happy memories of those days. Not every day was perfect; there were rainy days too, but it was good to be a child growing up in the 1920s. I have probably never shared all these memories with you before and am happy to do so now.

          Love,
          Mom

*Emily Jolley, raised in Highland Park, was trained as a secretary by a private tutor and was employed in the business office of Middlesex General Hospital for 44 years. Closely affiliated with the Reformed Church since childhood, she has sung in the choir for 70 years, served as elder, and was appointed church representative to Classis.*

# CAPTAIN TOLFSEN, MY GRANDPA

## Mildred Jones

Dear Kim,

Now that you have become a member of our family, I'd like to introduce you to an ancestor who gave up his seafaring life in Norway to settle in the United States of America. He was my grandpa, Captain Theodore Tolfsen.

I remember Grandpa as an old man with a bristly mustache and twinkly blue eyes. As youngsters, my sister, brother, and I would sit out on the back steps in the dark while Grandpa pointed out the stars. We learned to spot the Big Dipper, Orion's Belt, and the star so important to sailors, Polaris. As we grew older, he thrilled us with stories of his life at sea. His adventures seemed so romantic to me that I wondered why he gave up sailing and settled down to a life on land. But Grandpa never did become a landlubber, not really!

Theodore Tolfsen was born in 1855, in Gokstadin, Norway. As a little boy, he often played on Ghost Hill, a large mound near his home. One day he watched while some workers who were digging in the mound unearthed a Viking ship! Remarkably well-preserved, it peaked Theodore's curiosity, and he sneaked down into the dig and came away with a piece of a loose plank. This find turned out to be the famous Gokstad Ship that is now in the Oslo Museum. Grandpa's plank is a family treasure.

When young Theodore was 14 years old, his father, then a sea captain and part owner of his ship, was lost at sea along with his ship and entire crew. Like Herman Melville, young Theodore went to sea as a cabin boy to help in the support of his bereaved mother. At sea during the summer months, he continued his schooling in the winter, studying navigation. One summer, while aboard a small fishing smack, part of a fleet of 25 boats, a great storm came up near the Lofoten Islands in the North Sea. The hapless smacks were dashed against the rocks. Only two smacks survived, and Theodore was on one of them! At age 16, he worked his way across the Atlantic and found a job aboard a sailing ship in the Great Lakes. He enjoyed this experience and vowed to return some day. Back in Norway, his studies continued, and by his 19th birthday he had finished his courses and received his mate's license. At 21 years, he taught navigation for a while. Then as captain, he took command of his first ship. Called a barque, it was a three-masted, square-rigged cargo trading vessel with a crew of about 25. Later Grandpa showed us on a map where they sailed. Those sturdy cargo ships plied the seas to ports in Northern Europe, Iceland, North America, and the Caribbean. Grandpa told us that his favorite port in the whole world was New York Harbor.

These voyages were always dangerous. With only wind and ocean currents to propel the ships, with no radios, of course, and only a compass, sextant, barometer, and stars to guide him, Captain Tolfsen always managed to bring his ship to safe harbor. He braved the gales of the North Sea, icebergs, cyclones, and hurricanes in the Atlantic and rocky reefs along the coastlines. As captain of one of these relatively small though sturdy ships, he alone was responsible not only for the ship, but also for every member of the crew. He told us that he and his mate routinely served as physicians, sewing up wounds and setting bones of sailors hurt in the rigging during storms, as a chaplain who conducted services, as father confessor to homesick boys or frightened young sailors, and as peacemaker when fights broke out among sailors after endless months at sea. He told us he never had a chance to perform a marriage ceremony. There was never much chance of that aboard a trading vessel!

Then life changed for Theodore. He saw a small, dark-haired girl at a party one day, and, as Grandpa told us, "She was the one!" He and Henrietta Marie married in 1884. Henrietta Marie was the daughter of a ship owner who had died abroad but not at sea. Grandma told us that her father's sea chest had been sent home to her mother. In it was a dried orange. He had died of a tropical disease contracted while on shipping business in the Caribbean. Henrietta's mother took the pits from the orange and planted them. She grew an orange tree which remained in her parlor for the rest of her life.

That same year Theodore took command of a larger new barque named Sjufna at Londonderry, North Ireland. From this port to Baie Verte in Nova Scotia, he brought his vessel across the Atlantic in 17 days, fighting headwinds all the way—thereby breaking a shipping record. Other ships making the same trip required six weeks. Grandpa and the ship's owners made many profitable runs. Grandpa became well-respected in Northern Europe. However, a short time later, the Sjufna was sold, and Grandpa had to surrender his command in Sandefiord.

Realizing that sailing trade ships were being taken over by tramp steamers and such, Grandpa, with Henrietta and their new baby Aasta (my mother), decided to go to America to seek a new life in a new land. So in 1889, 34 year-old Theodore, wife, and child left Liverpool, England, aboard the Cunard Line, S.S. Umbria, bound for the port of New York. They settled in Port Washington, Long Island, and later moved to Westerleigh, Staten Island. Grandpa worked for a yachting company, testing and ferrying yachts to rich patrons on Long Island. Later, he worked for the New York City Department of Docks and Ferries. He was back at sea again, not with sails, but on small engine-driven harbor boats.

He and Grandma had seven children, but none of them followed the sea. However, my brother Howard inherited sea fever!! He is past Commodore of the Richmond County Yacht Club and has spent his vacations taking long trips on his 40-foot sloop to explore the waterways and coastlines from Maine to Florida.

In retirement, Grandpa maintained a ship captain's cabin in his basement. There he kept his sea chest, compass, his ocean and star charts. Every day he wrote in his log, studied the stars, and forecast the weather. For a long time he was able to watch the shipping in Lower New York Bay from Todd Hill in Northern Staten Island.

So Kim, your Great-great-grandpa never really left the sea, did he?

Love,
Grandma Jones

*Mildred Jones, though a native of New Jersey, spent much of her early life on Staten Island, New York. Always interested in early childhood education, she graduated from Booklyn College, studied further at Rutgers University, and is now a retired kindergarten teacher in the Borough of Metuchen. Married to a journalist, she is the mother of two sons.*

# THE NINETEEN THIRTIES

# CHRISTMAS FLASHBACKS

## Lorraine Bachman

Dear Jenna,

You asked me what Christmas was like when I was a little girl. The first story happened seventy years ago. You are only ten years old now, Jenna, and I expect you are surprised I remember something that took place so long ago.

What is the very first thing you remember about Christmas? That is the question I asked myself, Jenna. I was four years old. We had moved into the little house by the church. My older sister Martha went to school every day, and I had a new baby sister. I'm sure I was four years old because I am four years older than Jeanette. I was lonely. Martha had deserted me to go to school. I didn't know anyone to play with because I was living in a new house, and Mother was always busy taking care of Jeanette. I had a small table by the kitchen window where I would play, but I really spent a lot of time looking out the window and watching for Aunt Pauline to walk by. Back then, women would walk to the store almost every day to do their shopping. Aunt Pauline knew I was looking for her, and most every day she would come in to play with me. Mom told me that I would cry if she passed by without stopping. Jenna, I'm sure you can imagine—if a four-year-old child would watch for you every day and she would cry when you didn't come to see her—you would be sure to stop, too. Aunt Pauline was my favorite person, so it is natural that the first Christmas I remember is connected with her. I remember the Christmas present she gave me. She had made it especially for me. It was a gingerbread boy. This wasn't a cookie. It was a loaf of bread with a fat belly, head, arms, and legs. In my mind's eye, I can still see the raisins he had for his eyes and the raisin buttons on his chest. It was the best bread I had ever eaten. This is my earliest Christmas memory.

Let's jump ahead three years. Then I was seven and in the second grade. This was a Christmas event that happened in April— or maybe it was May. Our teacher asked everyone to tell his or her favorite story. I couldn't wait until it was my turn. When you are seven years old, you are eager to stand up in front and be the center of attention! I don't remember anyone else's favorite story, but I remember mine. It was the second chapter of Luke in perfect King James English, starting with the first verse—"And it came to pass in those days," and ending with the twentieth verse, " . . . and the shepherds returned glorifying and praising God for all the things that they had heard and seen, as it was told unto them,"—not missing one verse along the way. Jenna, it was my favorite story then, and it is still my favorite story.

The last Christmas memory took place when I was in eighth grade. By now I couldn't memorize as easily as I did when I was seven years old, and I would get nervous when I had to do anything in front of the class. However, I wouldn't admit that, so when I was asked to sing the second verse of "Silent Night" at our class Christmas party, naturally I said yes. I practiced hard. The family must have gotten tired of hearing me sing—"Silent Night, Holy Night, Shepherds quake at the sight," but I was sure I would remember every word. Well, the day of the party finally arrived, and the moment came when I was up front to sing the second verse. Jenna, do you think I will tell you I forgot the words? If so, you are wrong. I sang it all the way through, and I thought it was pretty good. Afterwards, no one mentioned it. I waited and waited. At last, when I was walking home with my best girl friend, I couldn't keep quiet any longer. "How did you like my song?" I asked. "Lorraine, you sang so quietly, no one could hear you!" she replied.

Jenna, Christmas is full of wonderful memories from that gingerbread boy right up to today. However, the most marvelous Christmas event took place two thousand years ago when "God so loved the world that he sent his only begotten son, that whosoever believeth in Him should not perish but have everlasting life." (John 3:16) Jenna, that is the greatest Christmas story of all!

       Lots of love,
       Aunt Lorraine

*Lorraine Bengston Bachman, born in Kane, Pennsylvania, was one of a contingent of only two women then studying accounting at Robert Morris College in Pittsburgh. After a few positions, she and her husband came to Edison in 1957. She has been active in the First Presbyterian Church and a volunteer with the Meals On Wheels program.*

# MEETING THE FAMILY AT AGE TWENTY-FIVE

## Hildegard Gerson Goodenough

Dear Children,

At twenty-five years of age, the only relatives outside of my immediate family that I had ever seen were two great uncles, brothers of my maternal grandfather. I had never laid eyes on a grandparent, aunt, uncle, or cousin! Married almost two years, this seemed a good time to go to Germany to meet my kin. And so, on July 30, 1932, I sailed for Hamburg, where I was welcomed by my cousin, Katharina Gerson, and her mother, widow of my Uncle Otto Gerson.

I became acquainted with them and their beautiful international port, with its well-known Alster Lake, Hagenbeck Zoo, Rathaus (city hall), and old churches and was delighted with both family and city. Then I went by train across part of northern Germany to visit my father's oldest sister, Elisabeth Gerson. She was a retired governess, living in the little town of Prenzlau. I remember particularly her quaint house with garden, the walks through the parks, and the fourteenth-century Marienkirche (St. Mary's Church).

Then to Stettin, where my father's younger half-sister Gertrude lived with her husband, Alfred Cochius, and their youngest son Heinrich. The other boys were away at school; and the daughter, two years older than I, was in South Germany. I met her thirty-three years later when I again saw my aunt and met one of the older boys.

Stettin is a lovely inland port on the Oder River, and we enjoyed the boat ride past banks colorful with flowers, saw some of this busy but clean harbor, had coffee on the Hakenterrasse, and took walks. Then again came the sad time of parting, for when would we meet again? Europe seemed a great distance from New York in 1932.

Next came a visit to my maternal grandmother, the only grandparent remaining. After having lived most of her life in Kuestrin, where her ancestors helped found the city seven centuries earlier and which is now in Poland, my grandmother and one unmarried daughter moved to the little village of Eisenhammer in the country. Another aunt and her eleven-year-old daughter were there during my stay; and the aunt from Berlin, a childless war widow, joined us for part of these two weeks. It was a restful time: breakfast at any hour, dinner at about noon, coffee and cake in the afternoon on the veranda, supper at seven, walks in the woods in the morning and late afternoon to pick blueberries, mushrooms, and green hazelnuts—which, by the way, were tasty. It was a wonderful experience, meeting my grandmother, with whom I had corresponded even as a child to thank her for gifts sent before the First World War. (My father had taught me to read and write German script before I started to school at the age of six.) Some of the people in this little village had never been far from home, and many questions were asked about New York City, where I lived then, and about my trip over the great ocean. They could not picture a ship big enough to live on for a week. The little girls always curtsied when we met on the road.

More sad farewells, for we were sure we would not meet again. Then on to Berlin, where my Aunt Marie was awaiting me. What a round of sight-seeing in those five days! All the benefits of my restful two weeks in the country disappeared in a short time, but I had to keep up with my aunt, who seemed to have boundless energy. She was determined that I should see all there was to see in Berlin. No museum or monument was missed, and there were many. I also enjoyed our walks down the Kurfuerstendamm and Unter den Linden and everything about that happy city. We, of course, also saw the palatial Reichstag and had coffee one afternoon outdoors at the Tempelhofer Airport. Even then a plane came into or departed from this airport every six minutes.

In Berlin I also met an older brother of my father, a tall, handsome retired teacher, and one of his daughters who was married to an American-educated Jewish dentist. At their house we ate kosher as his father, a rabbi, and his mother were with them. I missed another daughter by two weeks. A physician herself, she was married to a Turkish doctor, whom she met at medical school in Leipzig. She still lives in Istanbul.

My Aunt Marie came to Dresden by train with me, and we visited two outstanding museums, the Zwinger and Das Gruene Gewoelbe (the green vault). She returned to Berlin, and I went on to Frankfurt and Mainz, where the next morning I boarded the *Bismarck* to spend a day going down the Rhine, which is north. The all-day trip took me past castles high on the vineyard-covered banks of the river, recalling legends connected with many of them. It was an unforgettable day, which I was fortunate enough to repeat twice in the sixties.

Disembarking at Cologne, I took a train to Bochum, where my mother's oldest sister and her husband, Paula and August Mueller, met me. Here again we enjoyed a few days of sight-seeing conducted by a friend of my uncle, a teacher in the school; the trip included a tour through the mining university with its simulated coal mine.

During my stay, we walked through the parks, stopping for coffee, once in a castle which had been converted into a coffee house—overlooking the Rhine, of course.

My visit with relatives had ended, and I was pleased to claim such friendly, well-informed, and handsome people as my kinsmen. Another World War decimated the family, but I was privileged to meet some of them and some of the newer generation more than three decades later.

With love,<br>Mother

*Hildegarde Gerson Goodenough (d.1977) was born and raised in Pittsburgh and worked as a secretary at General Cable Corporation in New York City. She married and moved to Metuchen in 1935, where she raised three children, was active in the Presbyterian Church, volunteered with the Red Cross during World War II and in Roosevelt Hospital, and served as president of the Quiet Hour.*

# NEW YORK SCHOOLDAYS

## Gloria Marino

Dear Jessica,

I'd like to tell you about growing up in Queens in New York City during the era which was known as the "Depression" (economic, that was).

My parents owned a two-family house in Ridgewood, Queens. We lived on the first floor, and a series of tenants lived upstairs. The neighbors were predominantly first-generation Americans of German extraction—skilled workers and craftsmen. The street was the children's playground, supervised surreptitiously from behind lace curtains. We played games of stickball, giant steps, hide and seek, and ringalevio. As girls, we made our own paper dolls, were taught to crochet supplies of potholders from bakery string and to embroider gardens of flowers on household linens. We window-shopped on Myrtle Avenue and thoroughly explored Woolworth's. The public library was a short walk away, and I believe I read all the books in the children's section. On Saturday mornings the librarian held story hour and narrated great classic children's tales.

In the winter we made mountains and igloos of snow at curbside, from which we threw snowballs at the boys. I sang in the Junior Choir at the Methodist Church, and before choir practice we arrived early enough to become experts at jump rope. Every Sunday morning the choir sang at a service which was conducted in German. I remember the pastor thundering hefty German gutterals from the pulpit.

None of us had any feeling of deprivation or envy of the rich. The only wealthy people we knew were in the movies.

In summer the elementary schoolyard became a supervised playground. We performed in plays, wove lop-sided baskets and, of course, played ball. The giant wooden blocks were unavailable to girls, since the boys, always the enemy, brooked no interference with their elaborate construction. Every summer I went to visit my Aunt Sarah, Cousin Bessie, and Uncle George. Uncle George was superintendent of a large estate on Long Island. There were horses and many small wild animals I never encountered in the city. There were formal gardens, lawns, landscaped bridle paths, and several ponds. I went fishing in the ponds for sunnies and caught them by the dozen. They went into a pail of water for observation, and then I threw them all back in the water. I didn't want them to die.

From my Aunt Sarah and Cousin Bessie, I learned to make jams and jellies and to can other fruits and vegetables from the kitchen garden. In the evening I went to the "big house" downstairs and learned to play dominos and pinochle with the staff—the butler, the cook, the chauffeur, and maids. When the owning family was not in residence, I wandered through the "big house" to inspect the furniture, the paintings, the bibelots, the dishes, and the glassware. I was unintentionally getting an education for the eye. Their library was boring to me; all the books were about sailing.

The most rewarding years were those at high school. The teachers were remarkable people who were glad to be employed. We had both male and female PhD's in math, Latin, English, and languages. The teachers also supervised after-school clubs and activities, and I spent many hours playing competitive badminton. Through the efforts of the music teacher, my best friend and I got tickets for the Philharmonic performances at Carnegie Hall. In the summer, the Philharmonic also performed outdoors at Lewisohn Stadium at City College, and for fifty cents we sat on the stone bleachers. The high school Art Department got us tickets to the Student Arts League lectures at museums all over the city. We went to theater on our own.

On nice days we explored zoos and botanical gardens and rode the ferries. At Forest Hills Stadium, we attended tennis matches up to quarter finals. Best of all, we rode the trolley car to the World's Fair several times a week!

This describes New York City in the past, when young people could move around safely on transit systems and be home by 10 PM. When you smile at my colloquial New York accent, I smile too. I own it with affection. Of course, there were downsides—endless money worries and penny pinching, but for young people, the city offered priceless riches of the mind and spirit.

Much love,<br>Gramma

*Gloria Marino attended Brooklyn College and moved to Metuchen with her husband, who was a chemical engineer, and lived in the area for many years. Always active in church and community, she worked as Production and Inventory Control Planner at Revlon prior to her retirement, during which she pursues her many interests in music, literature, politics, and tennis.*

# BLIZZARDS AND HOBOS

## Elinor McCann

My dear Grandchildren,

As we enter a new year, a new century, and a new millennium, I am nostalgic about times past and am excited about all these new eras we are now entering. As I reflect on the many changes that define my life, I remember when you were small, you would ask me to tell you a bedtime story about my life as a child. Let me tell you another story about the traditional responses of people toward one another.

Our family gathered around the piano as Mother played and we sang favorite tunes. Winter winds howled through swaying boughs of ancient oaks, and snow was drifting across the landscape outside. We had reached the final phase of our family routine, preparing for children's bedtime.

This routine began by a parent reading aloud from the book currently being shared. Sometimes it was an adventure from the likes of Tom Sawyer or Huckleberry Finn, and other times it was sharing the sorrows of David Copperfield or Elsie Dinsmore. There were others—Pollyanna and Alice, or the wild goings-on in *Treasure Island*. Only much later did I learn how adept my parents were at cleaning up the language of some of the characters and toning down their more gory escapades. Some were so much more exciting when I read them myself a few years later.

We were into the last song when there was a loud, pounding knock at the door. As my father opened the door, a large, strange man stumbled in. He wore only a thin jacket, no hat, no gloves, and no boots. Great mounds of snow hung from his hair and especially his eyebrows as he stamped his feet and shook his shoulders, shedding the blankets of snow onto the floor. He asked for a cup of coffee!

Mother rushed to the kitchen as Father ushered him to the fire. He was pale and shivering; his teeth chattered as he rubbed his hands together over the fire, soaking up the warmth of the room. We four children, all under ten years of age, crowded together, wide-eyed, on the piano bench.

In the early 1930s, it was a common occurrence to have a "tramp" come to our door asking for food. Mother never turned them away. She prepared whatever was available at the moment, and the men sat on the back porch, ate, expressed their appreciation, and walked away. It had become an interesting interlude in the course of our lives in spring, summer, and fall, but never at night—and never in winter!

Our home was on a Missouri farm, a bit more than a mile out of town on First Street. A US highway ran along the edge of town, and the railroad was nearby. Men moved along these routes looking for employment, a place to move their families to start again. They came from all parts of the country during those desperate days of the Great Depression. When Father was home, he often engaged those men in conversations. They spoke of their families left behind, of the places they had lived or had passed through in their long search for a better life. We children were permitted to listen to some of these tales but were never to interrupt.

As our visitor began to be warmed, he took a chair near the fire. Mother brought in a steaming cup of coffee, a large bowl of beef stew, and fat slices of homemade bread. Those leftovers from our evening meal were quickly eaten as we children watched in amazement. When Mother offered more, he graciously declined.

My father raised cattle, horses, and Missouri mules on our farm. He also raised hybrid seed crops, cooperating with an experimental program developing grains that would be pest and drought resistant. On this particular evening he had made arrangements with a livestock trucker to come for a load of cattle. They would be at the Kansas City stockyards in time for the morning auction. When our visitor said he was going to Kansas City, my father suggested that, if the truck could come through the snow, he was sure the driver would be happy for his company. The man quickly rose from his chair and moved toward the doorway saying, "Oh, no, I can't do that. I can't wait. Your trucker may not be able to come through this storm."

As Father followed him, insisting the trucker would have called if he were not coming, the man prepared to leave. My father began to search out an extra stocking cap, gloves, and tattered heavy coat and scarf, insisting the man wear them. The man accepted the proffered clothing, wrapping himself as he stepped out into the frigid night. The angry winds gusted around him, and he was almost out of sight in the swirling snow when he fell sprawled in the drifts.

My father struggled, dragging the man into the house once again. I screamed, "Daddy, don't touch him; they'll get your finger prints!"

It had long been a practice that my father would gather the children around as he reviewed the daily newspaper. He would read and explain the affairs of the world as best could be done with such a young audience. The Lindbergh baby kidnapping and ensuing investigation were then in progress. The trial preparations, accusations, and speculations filled the daily news.

The man being dragged into the door looked perfectly dead to me, and I was terrified that my father would be accused of killing him! However, in a foggy daze, the man drank another cup of coffee as Mother gathered and herded us children off to our rooms and to bed. Some minutes later we heard the door open and then close. Father came into our rooms, telling us "goodnight" and assuring us the man had recovered and was off on his journey again.

Next day it was reported that an escaped convict had been captured a few miles from our house, trudging along the ditch of the highway, bundled in my father's coat. It became an oft-used warning when curious children around our house moved too near a questionable subject or crisis, "Don't touch it; they'll get your fingerprints!"

This is not a likely incident to happen today. We have organized our society so that agencies take care of people in need, and we don't feed strangers at our doors. I do wonder, with all the good reasons for changes in our society, if we haven't lost our personal compassion and involvement with individuals.

I do want to wish each of you great happiness in the new year!
With love,
Nana

*Elinor McCann spent her youth on a Missouri farm at the edge of a noted turn of the century health spa. She was a teenage teacher during World War II, an accountant, and a cartographer. Her husband's work brought about a move to the New York City area in 1956. She is the mother of two children.*

# ROADS WELL TRAVELED

## Virginia Okell

My dear Little Sister,
    I thought you might like to read the result of our "Remember when?" session of a few weeks ago. I am sending you part of the reminiscence I wrote for our Quiet Hour Club; perhaps it will stir up a few more memories, and we can have another session! I titled it "Innocents A-Road." Hope you enjoy it!

\* \* \* \* \* \* \*

I love road books—road movies; even a road map can give me a boost. In our family we try never to return on the same road by which we came, even if it's a choice between Route 1 and Route 27! There is adventure on the road—something to learn, something to laugh at, something to treasure. The road and I have been friends all my life.
    I have vivid memories of automobile travel as a child; we lived in Brooklyn, and our grandparents and assorted aunts, uncles, and cousins lived in the then-foreign lands of New Jersey and Connecticut. New Jersey was a day trip adventure; we got to choose whether to take the ferry or the Holland Tunnel to travel the plank road through the Meadowlands to the highlands of Montclair. It was exciting to see the trucks chugging onto the ferry or tooling along the road, bringing produce and live chickens from the farms into the waterfront markets and warehouses in Manhattan. Coming home on Christmas nights, we sometimes detoured to see the wondrous display of lights on the houses along Wyoming Avenue in South Orange.

Traveling to Connecticut was altogether a different adventure; it was at least a four-hour trip from Flatbush to Pine Orchard, just east of New Haven on the Long Island Sound, where our grandparents lived—no day trip, that! It was before the days of parkways and interstates: no Triboro Bridge, no Whitestone Bridge, no Merritt Parkway. Family suitcases were packed and strapped to a luggage rack on the rear of the car; in summertime our two-wheeler bikes were strapped on the running board. (Remember those?!)

Many of the trips were made at night, probably to ensure full days in Pine Orchard. A pair of sofa cushions would be placed on either side of the hump on the rear floor of the car to make a fairly level area. My sister, two years younger than I, and I would draw straws for the privilege of using the seat. The loser got the floor, and therefore less visibility. The parental hope was, of course, for sleeping children—but there was so much to see! We would go across one of the bridges (a choice, squabbled over, between the Brooklyn Bridge and the Manhattan Bridge); there were ships to see in the harbor—Navy vessels, sometimes at the Navy Yard, freighters docked at the United Fruit Company piers in lower Manhattan, and ferries in all directions.

Driving north through the city, we could glimpse open markets under the elevated railways. There were pushcarts piled high with all manner of goods and exotic shops patronized by exotically dressed people. It was an era when gypsies camped in vacant stores during the winter. We were thrilled to spot some of these colorful and mysterious people: women and little girls in long full skirts and shawls, flashing bracelets, and dangling earrings; men in black trousers and bright shirts, and some were wearing earrings! If we were driving at night, we sometimes rode up Broadway and gasped at the lighted signs, gleefully spelling out their messages to each other and wondering how the smoke rings came out of the Camel sign! Our mother smoked Camels sometimes, and our dad could blow beautiful smoke rings.

It was Post Road all the way. We knew the names of the towns, and when we drove past the United Illuminating plant in New

Haven and crossed over the bridge that our grandfather would cross every day on his way to work, we finally spotted the dairy farm atop the hill in Branford and knew we were *almost* there! The anticipation—of the ride, of the visit with grandparents and cousins, and of the freedom in playing in the rocky woods and along the shore of Long Island Sound—is something I can still feel.

The summer of my tenth birthday, I accompanied my parents on my first real grown-up trip. My sisters were left in Pine Orchard, and I—the chosen one, the grown-up—drove to Cape Cod with Mom and Dad. My memories of that trip include a ferry ride across Narragansett Bay at a time when the United States was building its defenses with an eye on war in Europe. The Bay was full of Navy ships, and there was an enormous amount of activity: small boats scuttled back and forth; officers' launches were everywhere; stores were laded aboard huge ships; and signs warned us that no picture taking was allowed. It was my first sense of something happening, something beyond my Brooklyn, Montclair, Pine Orchard world of childhood safety.

My further memories of that trip include an overnight stay in a tourist cabin. (Remember those?) These particular cabins were quite new and were shaded by tall trees. Mother approved the nice new wood smell. A cot was brought in for me, and we washed up and went to Howard Johnson's for dinner. Returning to our cabin, we turned down my cot and found it full of life. "Leeches!" shrieked Mother. Furious, my father headed for the office. Closed! All cabins taken. No one around. I shared the double bed with Mom after we carefully checked for wildlife. My 6'4" father did the best he could in the car. *I* slept well!

When we returned to Pine Orchard, I found my sisters and my cousins bubbling about their activities; all of them had been swimming and had built a raft, which sank—giggle giggle! I felt supremely superior and adult. *I* had traveled and had had adventures!

★ ★ ★ ★ ★ ★ ★

Please bear in mind, Ann, that this was written to be read aloud . . . ergo the sometimes odd punctuation. I'll call you soon to see if you have remembered more about those "olden days"!

        With much love,
        Big Sister Gin

*Virginia Okell was born in Brooklyn, spent her teens on Long Island, lived and worked in New York City after marrying a journalist, and ended up in Edison, where her three children were raised. A graduate of Connecticut College and Rutgers, she spent many satisfying years as a librarian at the University of Connecticut, the New York City Bar Association, and the Rahway Public Library.*

# THE LITTLE CHURCH

## Jane Palmeter

Dear Charles,

For some time you and I have talked about how we are members of the last "unprogrammed generation" and have thought seriously about writing about our childhood experiences as part of that generation. I have already written a couple of chapters in what may someday be put together as a book for our children and grandchildren. My thought is to introduce each chapter with reference to a hymn, a song, or other piece of music which had significance to us as we were growing up. When I say "we," I'm thinking of you and Jim and myself. The following is the chapter I've written on the "Little Church," which came into being under your guidance.

\* \* \* \* \* \* \* \*

"What a friend we have in Jesus, all our sins and griefs to bear! What a privilege to carry everything to God in prayer." I rose to sing with the rest of the congregation at First Presbyterian Church in Metuchen. The choir was standing in their blue robes outlined against the white paneling, and above them the minister in the pulpit looked out over the congregation. Suddenly, I was not there. I was in an old, converted chicken coop playing a pump organ and listening as other children's voices sang out clearly: "O what peace we often forfeit, O what needless pain we bear, All because we do not carry everything to God in prayer!" It was cold and damp, but we were bundled up and didn't seem to mind. This was our church, a children's church.

Let me take you back to the waning days of the Depression, to the year 1938, to a small town in northern Pennsylvania—Canton, to be exact. Our family lived in what now would be called a mixed neighborhood, but we recognized it only as our neighborhood.

A number of our playmates lived on the Lower Mountain Road. Their families had been on relief for years. Although my brothers and I attended Sunday School regularly, none of these children did. Their parents were not inclined to take them; the children probably would have felt uncomfortable, for in those days the girls wore patent leather shoes and organdy dresses, and the boys wore white shirts and ties on Sundays. My brother Charles conceived the idea of having a children's church on Sunday afternoons where all the children would feel welcome. He was twelve years old at the time.

He enlisted the help of our younger brother Jim, me, and all the kids in the neighborhood to convert an abandoned chicken coop into a church. This building had been divided into three sections, as our father, who was in the feed business, had used it to experiment with different feeding rations for chickens. We got rid of the old feed bags and bins, scrubbed and cleaned the whole building, painted the windows with watercolors to simulate stained glass, and acquired chairs out of various attics. Charles bought an old pump organ for five dollars. Our parents brought a ship's bell to us from Cape Cod, and we were ready to open the doors to any children in town that would come.

Sunday after Sunday at two o'clock, the bell would ring and the children came. Usually, there were about twenty —sometimes more, sometimes less—of all ages from all economic backgrounds. The choir sat on chairs on what formerly was the roosting area for the chickens. Charles stood behind a table with another small table placed on top to resemble a pulpit, and I was at the organ. Jim was the sexton and rang the bell. We had Bibles, and Charles spent his allowance for Sunday School material.

One weekend our Aunt Bess was visiting our home with a friend of hers, Emilie Hall. When Emilie saw the "Little Church" and the children filing in, she asked if she might take some pictures and write a story for *The Elmira Star Gazette*, a newspaper for which she often wrote feature stories. We doubted that it would be of much interest to anyone, but there was certainly no harm in her taking a few pictures and writing a story. The children liked the idea of having their pictures taken, and probably Charles, Jim, and I did too, although I don't remember that part.

Well, the story was circulated by the Associated Press, and it was printed in papers all over the country. Suddenly, to our amazement, letters began arriving from everywhere, many of them containing gifts of money. One man sent enough money so that we could buy hymnbooks, one of which I still have and which contains all my favorite hymns. Another man sent enough money so that we were able to buy some old pews from a church on the mountain, and so it went.

One evening just as we were finishing dinner, the phone rang, and it was "Hobby Lobby" calling to see if we could come to New York and appear on their radio show. Our mother's first question was: "What do you advertise?" You can be sure that if it had been anything to do with liquor or tobacco, our participation would have been out of the question. Fels Naptha seemed to be an acceptable product, so Charles and I, accompanied by our mother, took the night train from Elmira to New York City. Two things about the program stand out in my mind: Helena Rubenstein, who was on the program, and the little pump organ they found for me to play. It was like a "camp" organ, and I am sure I did not play it very well.

Perhaps the thing that seems to have impressed our children most, out of all the publicity tucked away in their grandmother's desk, is that we appeared on the pages of *Life* magazine. It was in the letters to the editor on April 17, 1939.

It was really a little church, where we sang the familiar hymns, read from the scriptures, and where each Sunday Charles gave a brief message based on scripture. How much influence this had on the children that came no one will ever know. Those children are now responsible people in their various communities.

Over the years the church fell into disrepair, but recently Charles, following his retirement from teaching, has restored it as a family chapel.

* * * * * * * *

I think you will agree, Charles, that Mother and Dad never discouraged us in our many endeavors, nor did they try to tell us how to do things. They certainly allowed us freedom to develop our own ideas, some of which were not always great! We were, I am convinced, the last "unprogrammed generation." Please send me your comments.

With love,<br>Jane

*Jane Rockwell Palmeter grew up in Canton, a small, rural town in northern Pennsylvania. After graduating from Bucknell University, she taught school for a short time. She married Saxton Palmeter in 1947 and came to live in Metuchen, where they have lived for over 50 years raising two sons and a daughter. She has been active in the First Presbyterian Church of Metuchen as well as a number of organizations in the community. She has been an active member of The Quiet Hour Club for forty-two years.*

# BACKSTAGE DAUGHTER

## Marnie Smith

My dear little Marnie,

It is so wonderful to have you as the newest member of our family. We have waited a long time for you. It is fun for me to tell you some stories about your "Grammie Marnie" when she was a little girl because, unlike the other grandchildren, you haven't heard it all before. My early childhood was seen through a kaleidoscope of car and train windows because our family traveled all over the country. Your Great-granddaddy was an entertainer, and so we lived in many places. I used to keep track of the states, and we had been to 46 of the then 48 states while I was counting. I never went to the same school two years in a row. It was difficult always being the "new kid on the block," but we did make a lot of new friends and saw so many different places and things.

One day as we were on the road, we saw circus tents in the field. It was always fun to see that because my daddy would stop in a nearby town for the night. We would stay in a tourist home, or maybe a tourist cabin, and then we would go see the circus. I always thought everyone was beautiful in shiny costumes and so brave to do those wonderful tricks. The parade of all the stars and animals was thrilling, and the clowns were especially great. I loved the small car that drove into the ring, and then so many clowns would climb out. You would really wonder how they all fit in; then they would play tricks on each other, and everyone would laugh so hard. The beautiful ladies were grand when they would "fly" on the trapeze, and I would always hold my breath when they would let go and "fly" to the catcher on another trapeze.

Some of the circuses had "sideshows" with "freaks" as the performers. These were people with special talents. The ones I liked were the contortionists—people who could turn themselves into strange shapes, sometimes twisting into knots that looked like pretzels. One woman put nails into her tongue; that's when I fainted and woke up behind the tent with that same woman putting wet towels on my face.

Once when we visited Clyde Beatty, Great-grammie Mary put her hand in the big cage and petted one of his lions. He told her in no uncertain terms that that was dangerous because those lions were not always friendly with strangers.

I liked everything about the circus, especially the sticky cotton candy. However, the special treat always came after the show was over, and we would go behind all the tents to meet friends and visit them in their travel trailers. You see, Marnie, your Great-granddaddy, "Monk" Watson, had run away and joined a circus when he was a little boy, and he had learned how to be a clown and do the acrobatic tricks. So when we went to the circus, he always knew some of the entertainers. It was really interesting to meet them after the show. I remember visiting one beautiful lady in her trailer with her glittery costume hanging up and watching her take off her make-up. It was fun to see her become a real person again. We would get a visit around the tents and meet the other acts and all the animals. I liked to pet the elephants, but they would never let us too close to the lions and tigers.

When your Mama Mary was a little girl here in Metuchen, I took her, Aunt Laura, and Uncles Chuck and Bob to the circus tent that came to Edison. Of course, I thought it was the "thing to do" to go to the trailers afterward to meet the people. It was really fun because several remembered my father. Norma Davenport was the woman who worked with the big elephants, and she and I remembered each other from the time I lived in Texas. At that time she was a very young girl with the circus and was training with the elephants even then. I haven't been to a tent circus for a long time, but I hope you will have the chance to go to one someday. It is hot, sticky, smelly—but wonderful! That's the best place to have cotton candy, too!

It wasn't only the circus that was thrilling to us. Great-granddaddy was an entertainer all his life. He was Master of Ceremonies and Band Leader during vaudeville, and he was a magician on stage for years. Whenever we went to a show that had actors who knew my daddy, we always went backstage to meet someone in the cast. I remember going backstage in New York to meet Boston Blackie—and Bert Lahr when he was in a play there; you will know him as the cowardly lion in the "Wizard of Oz." He was very nice and glad to see his old friend. We even met the organist at Radio City Music Hall. Bob Hope still writes to Great-grammie each Christmas! One of the last times I went backstage to visit a friend was to see Harry Blackstone, Jr., in New York. We grew up together in Colon, Michigan, the "Magic Capital of the World." It was fun to meet his wife Gay and little daughter Belemy. He came out to Metuchen to see us the next time he was in New York.

There is a phrase, "Backstage Wife"; I guess I could be called "Backstage Daughter." Thanks for listening, Marnie, I will have many more stories to tell you.

Love and XO XO,<br>Grammie Marnie

*Marnie Smith, born in Detroit, Michigan, holds a degree in speech and hearing therapy from the University of Michigan. She has taught in public schools and has an abiding interest in genealogy and patriotic organizations, currently serving as a National Vice President General of the Daughters of the American Revolution. She and her husband came to New Jersey in 1950 and reared four children in Metuchen.*

# SUMMER IN THE COUNTRY

## Marian Stone

Dear Alice,

When last we were together, you asked me what it was like to spend my childhood summers in the old family farmhouse where you now live. When I was with you at Thanksgiving, I was struck by the changes that had taken place over all those decades! There you and your brother Peter sat at the computer playing a game in the room that is now known as the library. When I was your age, just eight years old, the room was called the "parlor," and it was one of only two rooms on the first floor and was set aside for entertaining guests. My main activity in the parlor was the playing of the victrola, hand-wound of course, and the records were ones discarded by my college-girl aunt, your great-grandmother.

I spent 16 wonderful summers at the farmhouse. My grandmother, whom I called "Mother," and Aunt Mary would spend the week in June before school closed packing for the season, and Mother's car was packed to the brim. The car was a high-standing, square, maroon Buick, which was affectionately known as "Big Bertha" to the family. Mother handled it expertly, as she had handled the family horse and carriage before that. The trip seemed long to me, as it took at least two hours; but my father said that when he was a boy, they went to the farm by horse and carriage, and it took two days with an overnight stop in a hotel in Somerville—and that he rode his bicycle all the way!

As we made the final approach to the farmhouse, the steep hills were a challenge to the car. The dirt road was narrow, allowing passage of only one car at a time, and it had forbidding gullies on each side. Many times we chugged part way up the hill, only to stall and roll back down again, but we always finally made it to the top successfully.

I was always excited when the farmhouse came within view, and Black Jack, anticipating our arrival, met us at the gate, always with a broad grin. He had arrived a month before we came and had "made garden," trimmed the shrubbery, mowed the lawn, and generally prepared the house for our arrival.

The house was much smaller than it is now but had several out-buildings. There were a barn, a woodshed, a toolshed, Jack's house, and an outhouse. You see, there was no electricity available on the mountain until the 1940s, and we had no indoor plumbing, as there was no running water. A hand-pumped well supplied our drinking water, and in times of drought the well went dry, and water had to be carted from neighboring springs, a job in itself.

There was a cistern at one end of the house where the breezeway is now. Every house had a cistern to collect rain water as it washed down from the roof. Cistern water was soft water, not the hard and icy cold water that came from the well and was used for laundry, for bathing, and for watering the garden. Strung near the cistern from one end of the house to the large pear tree was a hammock, one of three that hung in the yard. Hammocks were wonderful things—the best of all for relaxation, provided it wasn't the season for the pear tree to drop ripe pears whose juices would attract yellow jackets!

The summer stretched ahead gloriously when we arrived each June. Every weekend Papa, my grandfather, would arrive with guests, and games would be played both inside and outdoors. The men would compete in horseshoes and riflery, and in the evening there would be bridge games with tables set up in the parlor.

The Fourth of July celebration was the biggest day of the summer. Papa would bring firecrackers, including Roman candles, and after dark we'd sit on the front porch and "ooh" and "aah" as he set them off. Friends and family from all around would gather for the festivities. After the fireworks he would drive down the mountain to the little town of Bloomsbury and bring back quarts of ice cream, for which the confectioner was famous.

The nearest town, with its post office, grocer, bank, and drug store, was five miles away, nestled on the Delaware River. Shopping was an event. Lists were made out and trips to town were carefully planned. In town we purchased everything but milk and eggs, which were products of a nearby farm where we walked daily for our supply. When I was very young, I accompanied Mother on the trek each morning for milk, but when I was older, I went by myself, carrying an empty milk can and exchanging it for a full one when I met the farm girl (my good friend) halfway.

At least once a week, we went on some special expedition. For really big purchases we drove across the Delaware River to Easton and made a day of it. That city had a large open market, and townswomen came with baskets on their arms to carry their purchases. I loved to shop in Easton and always looked forward to having lunch at the YMCA cafeteria during each visit.

On really hot days we packed a picnic and drove down the hill to Sweet Hollow Road and settled there alongside the brook. We spread our blanket and ate our sandwiches and then went wading in the icy cold brook that raced along over a rocky path at the foot of the mountain. It was the best way in the world to cool off when the temperature soared.

We had a telephone to provide some connection to the outside world. The phone hung on the wall and had a hand crank to call the operator. It was a party line, and our signal was two short rings. We could hear signals for other people, too, but we were not to lift the receiver unless it was for us. The conversations were short. Invitations to friends or cousins could be made, recipes could be traded, doctors could be called to make visits should an illness appear: all could be done over the phone. It was an important device.

Labor Day was the sign that summer was over and plans must be made to leave and be ready to start school. No one wanted to leave, least of all me. Sometimes we would return for a fall weekend, for there was a black iron stove used for warmth and for cooking. All summer cooking had been done on a kerosene stove, and all light was provided by kerosene lamps, which had to be filled everyday.

Those summer days were happy days, and I look back on them fondly. I am glad that you and your family are happy living in that old farmhouse, too.

Love,<br>
Aunt Marian

*Marian Stone has lived in Middlesex County, New Jersey, throughout her life and has always been interested in New Jersey history. A graduate of Douglass College and Yale Univeristy, she has presented historic slide lectures extensively and serves as docent in two local house museums. The wife of a scientist for forty-four years, she is the mother of a son.*

# TRIPS ACROSS THE COUNTRY

## Caroline Towt

Dear Betsy,

You asked about my mother's trips to New Mexico during my childhood. Grandma Shelp had two sisters who lived in New Mexico. Aunt Caddie had gone there as a bride in 1913. Aunt Fan went to live with her sister in 1916, when my Grandmother Fordon died. All the other Fordon children graduated from high school in Geneva, New York; Aunt Fan graduated from high school in Roswell, New Mexico.

The families of the sisters visited each other in the summer. One year the family from New Mexico would come east, and the next year my mother and I would go to New Mexico.

Until 1936, we made the trip by train. Grandmother and I would take the New York Central train from Amsterdam, New York, to Chicago, Illinois. We would travel by Pullman car and have a lower berth. The two seats which faced each other would pull out to make a bed. The lavatories were at each end of the car. We had dinner at night in the dining car.

At Chicago, we had to change trains and railroads. During the stopover, we took a taxi to the Palmer House, a famous hotel in Chicago, to have dinner. I remember being so impressed because the waiter, a black man who wore white gloves, pulled the chair out for me.

We traveled on the Santa Fe Railroad to Clovis, New Mexico, and were on the train for two nights. The Santa Fe Railroad did not have dining cars. The train would stop in certain cities at restaurants called Harvey Houses. The train porter, called a "red cap," would come through each passenger car with a menu for the meal, and each passenger would make a selection. We would depart from the train and eat our meal in thirty to forty-five minutes. When it was time to return, the porter would ring a very large brass bell. The last part of the trip from Clovis to Roswell was made in a dirty coach train. That trip took about six hours.

Ever since 1927, the family from New Mexico made the trip east by car. I remember Uncle John (Aunt Caddie's husband) had a tan Buick, and Aunt Fan had a Ford with a rumble seat.

In 1935, Grandma Shelp had a new "Ford Victoria," and she decided to drive to New Mexico. My father was not too pleased with the idea. However, on July 5, 1935, Grandma Shelp, Happy our Boston terrier, and I left Amsterdam, New York, for Roswell, New Mexico. We stayed the first night in Geneva, New York, with Grandma's oldest sister Lucy. This was a familiar trip because my mother had driven Route 5 to Geneva and back to Amsterdam many times.

The next morning we left Geneva at about six in the morning and traveled on Route 5 to just east of Cleveland, Ohio. We stayed there on Tuesday night. There were no motels as we have today. We stayed in small individual cabins, usually kept by one owner. Sometimes these cabins were a second business for farmers who lived near the highway. There were no dining rooms, so we ate in "diners" which were in the small towns. Some of the time the roads were only two lanes. My mother always made it a point to stop traveling by four o'clock in the afternoon so we could assess the surroundings fairly. The third night we stayed near Vandalia, Illinois. At St. Louis we crossed the Mississippi River on the Chain of Rocks Bridge. Since you live in the area, you know how famous that bridge is, although it is no longer in use. From St. Louis we drove on Route 66 to Clovis, New Mexico. We stopped at night in Tulsa, Oklahoma, and the last night in Amarillo, Texas. Finally, on Saturday about noon, we arrived in Roswell. We were very glad to be there and very tired. I think the family in Roswell was relieved when we turned into their driveway. We made the return trip about the middle of August.

The road from Clovis to Roswell was not paved. It was about six lanes wide and made of gravel which had been plowed to make a hard surface. It was very dusty and dirty. On the trip we had only one flat tire. It was on the road somewhere between Clovis and Roswell. As my mother stood looking at the car, a farmer in a Ford truck stopped to help us. Mother wanted to pay him. I remember he looked at our license plates and said if his wife were ever in New York State, he hoped someone would help her. Both of us wondered if that really would have happened. Maybe, in 1935.

Betsy, you and I know your grandmother was a very gutsy woman, but when I think of her making that trip at age fifty-five under those conditions, I am always so proud of her.

In her later life when she came to live with us after your father died, she would fly to New Mexico to see her sister. I think she was always a little afraid of flying and enjoyed her driving trips more.

I do hope this letter has answered some of your questions.

                Much love to you.
                Mother

*Caroline Towt was born in the farming community of Amsterdam, New York. After graduating from Cornell University, she did graduate work at Columbia-Presbyterian Hospital in New York City. A widow with three children at age thirty, she continued her professional life in dietetics for thirty years and has lived in the Metuchen area for fifty years.*

# MY GRANDPARENTS' GENES

## Nancy Wright

My dear Grandchildren,

Twelve years ago I became a grandmother for the first time. Since then I have been blessed with two more of you. It's a special feeling that sweeps over a grandmother, and she realizes that her genes and possibly some of her particular interests may develop in these individuals whom she loves as her very own grandchildren. My thoughts recently have turned to my grandparents, and I have thought of their characteristics and interests. Do my life and my interests reflect any of theirs? I believe so.

My paternal grandfather was a doctor in Atlanta, Georgia. Although he died when I was 12, I can remember being fascinated with his medical books. Did this spark my interest in science? Over 100 years ago he bought a farm outside Atlanta in Cobb County. He and my grandmother lived there during their later years, as they were both very fond of country life and animals. I too enjoy the outdoors a great deal. For most of my life, a dog was present in my home. As my grandfather was being taken from his home on a stretcher several days before his death, he reminded his grandchildren to take care of the animals. At that time my horse was my prized possession.

Both he and my grandmother were serious people, and she particularly was a very devoted member of her church. Perhaps it came naturally, as her father and brother were Presbyterian ministers. I feel my faith is strong, and I have always enjoyed serving my church in various capacities. Also, Nana Crowe was a very ordered person. Her home, her kitchen, and her daily activities were very organized and neat. Am I? Most would say "yes," but there is always room for improvement. I do like the old adage, "A place for everything and everything in its place."

My mother's parents were devoted to each other. Grandpa Crane was much older than his wife. He died in the early 1930s, but my memories of him are very strong since we spent the greater part of each summer at their cottage on the Severn River outside of Annapolis, Maryland. Retired as comptroller of Bethlehem Steel, he was well-versed in numbers. I too enjoy the world of numbers, having been treasurer of various groups and the manager of our household accounts. He was a very jovial person and often had his grandchildren gathered round him while he told us funny stories.

Of my four grandparents, I was closest to my Nana Crane, perhaps because she lived until I was 27 years old. Several of my first cousins felt that she was almost mean. However, I found her warm, loving, firm, but very fair. She enjoyed handwork, and it was from her that I probably inherited my enjoyment of all types of handwork. As I recall, she was the one who taught me to knit. In her later years she was fond of traveling, and that too has been a strong interest in my life.

Life was a challenge for my grandparents. The world was changing rapidly for them, as it is for me today. They met the challenges and changes well, as I hope I am doing. Will you meet the challenges of your life with their strength, determination, and courage? I believe you will.

In these early years of your life, what interests and hobbies are you enjoying? When you are grandparents, how will you remember me? Besides giving you a never-ending abundance of love, what of my genes and interests will have played a part in your lives? May they be positive and constructive and give you now and always a sense of blessing and happiness.

My love always,<br>Granny

PS I must share with you the "bird" story of Crane-Crowe. My mother, Dorothy Crane, was introduced to my father, Walter Andrew Crowe, by a Mrs. Martin in Sparrows Point, Maryland. They were married by a Reverend Goodwin, who, my father claimed, blew the stork along. He was delighted when I married the "Wright" bird.

*Nancy Wright grew up in Georgia and graduated from Randolph-Macon Woman's College in Virginia. In 1943 she became the second female chemist hired by the DuPont Company. Most of her middle years were lived in Metuchen, where she raised two daughters and was active in the Quiet Hour Club and many other organizations.*

# SELF DISCOVERY

## Anna S. Young

Dear Mary Louise,

You mentioned how burdensome it sometimes felt to be the eldest. You said that when we were growing up, you felt responsible for the actions and failures to act of not just one Sherwood Girl, but of five. But there must have been some compensations.

As I chat with my granddaughter Joanna, I realize how thrilling it must be, at least sometimes, to be the first in a family: the first to read (how she loves to read!), the first to understand and work with math, the first to master any new skill. Right now Joanna is overjoyed when she can perform two-digit multiplication. "It's easier if you have lots of zeros—like, 20 times 40 is—um—um—800!" (Right! That's what I got, too.)

Being the youngest of five presented a mixed bag, too. You tell me that I was spoiled rotten, and you have often reminded me that I broke my glasses almost weekly as a kid and that Mom would replace them time after time after time with hardly a word of criticism, whereas you were expected to be perfect in all respects. But there was one heavy burden I bore as a small child, placed on my weak shoulders by relative strangers, the adult acquaintances of Mom and Dad that I would be introduced to from time to time, not people close to the family. They always knew what to say to the youngest: "It's too bad you weren't a boy. My, your father must have been disappointed!" I was a sensitive, obedient little twit, eager to please, and could do nothing about this apparent problem. Talk about responsibility! Dad didn't help the situation when he used to address me as "Mary Louise, Caroline, Barbara, Ruth, DAMMIT! Anna!"

I have no recollection of the day when I ran away, but the rest of you loved to tell the story, and I can't help but think it grew out of those "should have been a boy" remarks. I was about four years old, and you must have been eleven. I turned out to be missing, and Mom and Dad phoned the police and made a frantic search of the neighborhood. Pretty soon the police called and reported that they had located no missing girl children, but they did have a small boy at the station who, except for the chopped-off blond hair, seemed to answer my description. I never again tried physically to run away from the problem of being one girl too many.

Well, on reflection, it seems to me there was one person who had an idea of what I was going through as the youngest. There weren't many years that Grandma Sherwood and I had in common, but I can remember her when she appeared to me as alert, competent, and ever so comfortable to be with, much like the other adults close to us, but maybe even a little more comfortable sometimes.

On one occasion, I remember, I had apparently been delivered to her huge (to me) Victorian house (Remember the "Castle"?) for a couple of games of Parcheesi, a couple of radio soap operas ("Our Gal Sunday," "One Man's Family"), and maybe even the exchange of a few words. I don't remember the drive over to Grandma's or the involvement of anybody else, but just being there with her.

What suddenly caught my attention during that afternoon was a framed photograph on Grandma's desk of a blonde five-or six-year-old girl, not bad looking, almost pretty. Although she was smiling, you didn't notice the crowded front teeth, and the chin didn't recede noticeably. She was there on that desk all by herself, not in a group photograph, and not at the end of a stair-step series of pictures. I thought, "Oh, my goodness, that's me!" and, in a shy, furtive sort of way, I was actually pleased to be that girl.

So here we are, some sixty-five years later, still fussing like the Smothers Brothers ("Mom always liked you best!"). Do you suppose anybody ever gets over the birth-order thing? I don't suppose so, but I keep working on it.

Give my love to the "kids" when you talk to them, and to their kids. I'll never get used to Tom's no longer being there! Let me know if there's anything I can do to help. And don't forget to keep in touch!

Love,<br>Anna

*Anna S. Young was born and raised in Providence, Rhode Island. She attended Middlebury College, graduating with an AB degree in English literature. She married a man involved in construction engineering and proceeded to travel extensively while giving birth to four children. She and her husband and children settled in Edison, New Jersey, at the time the eldest started school.*

# THE NINETEEN FORTIES

# THREE

## Lynn Bergner

Dear Mom,

I have been asked by the teacher of my creative writing class to write of an event in my childhood that in some way altered my life. Since family has always been so important to you, I thought you would especially enjoy my reminiscences of how family members, old and new, played a part in my third birthday. So, here's my story!

\* \* \* \* \* \* \* \*

"I'm three, I'm three, today I'm turning three" was all I kept thinking. You're probably wondering how can anyone of decided middle age remember her third birthday. It did take place more than a half century ago! Keep reading, please.

It was June 13, 1944, and I awoke very excited with those very thoughts described above. It was my third birthday and the day of my very first birthday party—with friends of my own age, that is. I was told that I would even get presents. I was to wear my favorite brown dress, or "grown gress" as I liked to call it, and Mom would fix my hair in my favorite hairstyle. Please don't ask what a three-year-old was doing being preoccupied with hairstyles; I think I was peculiar. But I do remember; Mom would part my chin-length hair on the left side, make a braid on the right side, and fold the braid up to make a loop, which she clipped in place with a barrette. O.K. I'll admit to the fact that family stories and a few photographs helped in remembering the dress and barrette details. The rest really is mine.

Sometime in the early morning, however, there was a change in plans. Dad told me that Mom had to go to the hospital and that I'd be staying with Aunt Sarah. Aunt Sarah, the younger of Mom's two older sisters, was really my second mother. She was also the creator of the "braid coiffure." A baby nurse who loved children, she and Uncle Max were never able to have their own. I was lucky to be the one they pampered and indulged as if I were theirs. I was somewhat surprised, therefore, when Aunt Sarah became annoyed with me that I was expecting a party. A real one, I indicated, with guests my own age, who'd naturally be bringing gifts. Poor Aunt Sarah. How was she going to rustle a party together for me? She had no car nor did she drive. Here I was, putting her in the embarrassing predicament of asking similarly "vehicularly challenged" women to arrange for their daughters to come to my party, presents in hand, on that very day. Well, she did it, though I don't remember about the present part.

Each afternoon during the next ten days, Aunt Sarah and I would walk to Passaic General Hospital and wait on the street. At a designated time, Mom would appear at the window and wave to me. After waving back, Aunt Sarah and I would walk home. One evening, Dad stopped by and told me he'd be picking me up the next morning and that together we'd be bringing Mom home from the hospital. I was excited and, of course, couldn't wait to see her. Poor Dad! On arriving at the hospital in the pouring rain, he noticed that he had a flat tire. He explained to me that since he had to change the tire, he'd be sending Mom and me home in a taxi. Soon I was sitting in a taxi, and Mom was sliding into the seat beside me. She was holding my birthday present, all wrapped up, tightly next to her. She smiled as she showed me my baby sister, Bette, a.k.a. Betsy, and all I could think of to say was, "Oh Mommy, what a teeny, tiny piecer." (No memory here; more family lore.)

From that day forward, June 13 became the special day in our house. As our parents' only two children, it was the only birthday that was really celebrated. At our parties, there were the Betsy table for her friends and the Lynnie table for mine. People always asked if I resented having to share my birthday. I always answered "no" honestly, but I never seemed able to explain why. The day was never less special because I shared it; in fact, it was more special because it was shared. And what could have been a better gift?

So you see, it's easy for me to remember my third birthday. Firstly, the anecdotes were repeated to me many times over the years. And secondly, it really was, and continues to be, very special.

\* \* \* \* \* \* \* \*

Well, Mom, did you enjoy the story? I hope it made you smile to realize, firstly, how much I remembered about that day and also to see how much your giving me a sister has meant to me. I hope you are well and that I can visit soon. I'll call on Thursday.

Love,
Lynn

*Lynn Politt Bergner has lived all her life in New Jersey. Married, she is the mother of two grown sons and has earned the rank of Grandma three times to date. Lynn majored in foreign languages at Rutgers University and taught French and Spanish for twenty-six years in the Woodbridge Township School District. She is currently the owner of Franco-Files, where she works as a travel consultant planning personalized itineraries to France.*

# MY MOTHER—
# SHE KNEW HOW

## June Durkee

Dear Kim and Lisa,

    I am sending something to you that I wrote about "Bam," your grandmother, trying to describe her as I would to someone who didn't know her or us. I've thought a lot about her lately, and I especially want you, as young women, to remember what a special lady she was.

    When I was a child, a favorite question people liked to ask me was, "What are you going to be when you grow up?" I heard this many times from visiting clergy (who seemed to come to us regularly), relatives, and even casual adult acquaintances. It is only now, at this somewhat over-the-hill stage of my life, that I sincerely wonder why I was never asked instead, "HOW are you going to be?" I am sure that this is the real awe-inspiring, life-changing question to ask, and it reminds me of my mother. I want to tell you why.

    I became a "career woman" at age forty, shortly after the birth of my last child and right in the middle of the birth of the feminist movement. My becoming a working mother was not at all by choice. Rather, I joined the work force out of the necessity of having to raise five children on my own. After considerable scrounging around, I found myself with three part-time jobs, a briefcase, a commuter's train ticket, and a brand new outlook on life. I was in charge, I was PAID, I was fulfilled—I was hooked!

From then on, I am ashamed to say, I gradually began to assume a slightly condescending air when speaking about or with those members of my sex who continued to be content with their lives on the home front. However, because I was so busy running from one job to another as well as frantically trying to give "quality care" to five active, growing children, the only woman I ever got to talk to at any length was Mom. Once a week on Saturday or Sunday afternoon, I would walk across town to the house where I grew up and have my weekly visit with her.

There she would be sitting in the little sun-filled TV room, reading or knitting or working on the crossword puzzle from the daily paper. First, she would ask about each one of the children and then listen avidly to every little bit of news concerning them. The only thing she wouldn't tolerate was any slight hint of criticism of any of their doings. She loved each one of them unconditionally, absolutely, and each one of them knew it. They often went to visit her without any prodding from me. Not only that, they took their friends and acquaintances and always the latest boyfriend or girl friend—of whom she always approved. No matter that one boyfriend had a ponytail halfway down his back, a leather vest, and a scrubby beard. He was served tea and dainty cakes from her best china and given courteous attention by his hostess. How wise she was! And how funny! Though she was the picture of dignity and certainly what one would call the epitome of a lady, she had a wicked and even sometimes naughty sense of humor that my teenagers found hilarious. After all of us visited her one day, my son Mark observed, "It doesn't matter how bad we might be fighting in the car coming here, we always leave her house smiling."

Somehow, sometime in her life I think she just made up her mind to be cheerful. Not that she saw life through rose-colored glasses. She had plenty of opportunity to observe its painful realities. I watched her endure four long years of separation from her sons during World War II—one in the Atlantic and one in the Pacific. I saw her nurse my father through his last, long, painful illness. Mostly, I can still see her the morning after my husband's tragic death. She just appeared at our door, took the first chair in sight, and simply sat all day long. She was just *there*, and seeing her there somehow made us feel that someday, somehow, everything might be all right for us, too.

She refused to be pessimistic. As her daughter, this sometimes irritated me, but her gaiety was authentic and unassailable. Though she certainly never "preached" to us, she left no doubt as to where her strength lay. Her faith was simple and unswerving. Although she read most of the books on the *New York Times* bestseller lists, her day always began with reading THE book before anything else. One day after completing it for what would be the very last time, she closed it and said, "There. I don't believe I'll get all the way through again."

I don't mean to give the impression that she was a saint, because she wasn't. On occasion she had a sharp tongue which could be pretty cutting when dealing with those who fell into disfavor. I just mean that her presence in our lives, her wonderful example of what I think is meant by abundant living, she accomplished just by *being*.

So, I would sit and visit her, probably on the edge of my seat, since I was always in a hurry in those days. I, with my newfound importance as a real working woman, would wonder how she who had never "worked" a day in her life could be so fulfilled. I'm sure she never wondered what she was going to be when she grew up, but now I know she certainly had the answer as to *how* to be.

With much love to you both,<br>Mom

---

*June Potter Durkee grew up in Metuchen with all of her relatives. A graduate of the Eastman School of Music, she continued her studies years later at Rutgers University's Mason Gross School of the Arts. Returning to Metuchen, she raised five children while singing professionally in New York, directing choirs in New Jersey, and teaching.*

# POIGNANT RECOLLECTIONS

## Judith Hassert

My darling granddaughter Rebecca,

War is an earthshaking, devastating experience. Lives are changed and indelible impressions are left. It also ignites in young and old an idealistic longing to contribute in some way to a cause bigger than self.

When Grandpa received orders from the navy to report for fleet duty in the Pacific, I returned to my home in New Jersey, where urgent messages were waiting about my possible employment with the army. A librarian was needed in the hospital at Camp Kilmer. Soon I was being shown around this huge base, where personnel were both embarking and departing, and recreational activities were desperately needed. Hospital wards were burgeoning with patients who had everything from the lowly measles to complicated diseases and injuries. Some patients remained for a few days, while others remained many months. Others moved to larger, specialized hospitals. Principally, my job was to wheel a bookcart in and out of wards where soldiers were eagerly looking for something to occupy the time that was hanging heavily; in addition, they were happy to see a new face. But there was a somber, saddening part of the job. It became clear that some patients were too ill to recover and return to their homes.

The memory of one such soldier, as well as others, has always remained in a corner of my heart. His demeanor was somewhat retiring and quiet, but he was gratified to have someone listen to expressions of pride for Wales, his country of birth. It was obvious from his ashen color that his leukemia was serious, and, having learned that his wife and family had returned to Britain, I frequently stopped to see him. We chatted about how gifted the Welsh are in singing, and he asked if I would return with my autoharp and sing for him the beloved folksong, "All Through the Night." Singing comes from the deepest recesses of the heart, and it took every ounce of courage to keep my voice from breaking, knowing that the sacrifice he was making must have felt like a long and lonesome journey.

One day after lunch, a noisy group of young soldiers wandered into the library looking for some diversion. They were waiting to be shipped to a new overseas assignment. Among them was an especially handsome soldier with curly black hair and a freshly scrubbed appearance. Eventually, one of the group confided to me that this particular fellow was unable to speak. The psychiatric staff of the hospital was attempting to treat him for hysteria, and if they did not succeed, he would be given a medical discharge.

A casual observer might assume that a serviceman would be courageous enough to face dangers inherent in an overseas assignment, but there were many men who were not secure or self confident enough to withstand the fears that accompany the horror of battle on foreign ground.

Army service proved to be an intense course in growing up rapidly—a little akin to being branches from a forsythia bush brought indoors during the latter days of winter and forced into bloom. I was twenty-four years old at the time and had been married a short six months. This was my first encounter with life and death situations. In all probability, I was not mature enough to fully comprehend the insights and learnings I gathered during the war, but in retrospect I would not exchange those months. Being separated from loved ones changes one's priorities from trivialities to verities, and what a blessing it was when my husband and I could be reunited.

                              Love,
                              Grandma

*Judith Hassert, after a precarious entrance into the world with her twin sister, happily sang duets with her from kindergarten through Douglass College. After additional studies at Rutgers, she taught elementary school in both public and private schools. In a dual career, she also served in a variety of libraries. She, her research scientist husband, and two daughters resided for forty-one years in Metuchen.*

# A WAR-TIME REMINISCENCE WITH MY GRANDSON

## Mary B. Jones

Dear Alex,

I have been thinking about your phone call to us the other evening. We were so pleased to hear about your school project on World War II. Your Dad said you have taken quite an interest in the war. I listened intently as you interviewed your grandfather about his role in making the atom bomb in the very secret operation called the Manhattan Project. For an eleven year old, you asked such probing questions about uranium and its isotope U-235, about electrons and valences and such. When I was your age, I was poaching pollywogs from a nearby pond, collecting wildflowers, and chasing moths and butterflies.

Gramp sounded like a patient professor as he explained in clear and simple language even I could understand the chemistry and physics behind the research he did.

As I began to reflect on Grandfather's contribution to the war effort, I suddenly realized that I also did my part. It seemed so small in comparison to research or service in the armed forces that I dismissed it as inconsequential. I can now proudly say, "I too served." Your grandmother worked in a defense plant testing B-29 bomber engines. I was very young at the time, having just finished my freshman year at the University of Illinois. That summer there were frantic ads for defense workers, and since it was a good opportunity to earn money for college tuition, I applied. I think it was on the strength of my advanced high school physics course that I was hired.

We worked in teams of two in a makeshift hangar hastily converted into cubicles. Each cubicle had a thick plate glass wall separating the mounted behemoth engine from our operating panel. When I first glimpsed the eighteen-cylinder radial engine with two turbo superchargers, whatever they were, that delivered 2,200 horsepower at takeoff, I paled. To think there were four of these engines mounted on one plane! My father's '38 Chevy had six cylinders, and on a good day coughed up 100 horsepower.

My job was to record all the test data on a long log sheet. My co-worker, whom I called "pilot," was a married man with children, disqualifying him from serving in the army. He usually performed the acceleration and deceleration stages of the tests. It was very noisy, and we had to shout to each other. Oil consumption, RPM's, and other engine statistics were duly noted as well as any other minor repairs and adjustments. Calculations had to be made by me for the conversion to miles per hour and flight times. The signed log sheet accompanied each engine which passed the test procedures when it was shipped to an assembly plant somewhere in the USA. Silently, I prayed for the young Air Force pilot who would fly this four-engined Superfortress.

Except for pictures, I never saw a fully assembled bomber. I couldn't even imagine its size. It had a wingspan of some 141 feet, a length of almost 100 feet, and it towered nearly 28 feet above the ground. The B-29 Superfortress was used in the Pacific theater of war. Its great range of 4,000 miles made it well suited for flights over water. Its maximum speed of about 350 mph and its ability to fly above 30,000 feet made it useful in the attacks on Japan from bases in Guam and China.

That's my story, Alex. What a curious coincidence that long before I met Grandfather, it turns out that he took part in developing the atom bomb, and I tested engines for B-29 bombers, one of which dropped the bomb on Japan, ending the war.

I wish you well on your school project. Keep us posted.

Love,
Gram

*Mary B. Jones grew up in a bucolic village near Downers Grove, Illinois. There she began a life-long love affair with nature. She attended the University of Illinois. After her marriage to a research scientist, she transferred to New York University. A resident of Metuchen for 49 years, she raised four children.*

# A SPECIAL YEAR OF MY LIFE

## Gerda Woerner

Dear Friends,

While World War II was in progress, my husband Irv was assigned to a Marine base adjacent to Camp LeJeune, North Carolina. He was a professional architect whose knowledge was needed in a particular phase of ship design.

We had been married about a year at the time, and I was to accompany him to his new assignment, located in the very small town of Jacksonville, near Camp LeJeune. We were overwhelmed by the sights that greeted us in Jacksonville!

To our great surprise, throngs of people had descended on the tiny town, and there seemed to be no place for us to live; in fact, the situation was so serious that householders were renting their front yards, setting up tents as their living quarters. Some lucky people had trailers! Well, we were lucky, too. The owners of a grand, newly built house rented us their master bedroom with our very own private bathroom. We felt we were living in luxury.

While my husband was very busy, I found I had time on my hands and cast about for something to do. Our very accommodating landlady suggested I join her as a volunteer in the American Red Cross office right in town. I jumped at the chance to be active and useful. The Red Cross office director, a very capable woman some years my senior, seemed to like me, and we developed a pleasant relationship rather quickly. She was a typical Southerner, with a deep drawl; quite in contrast, I was a Northerner who hailed from Hackensack, New Jersey, and I suppose I had my own accent for her to listen to. My post-college Katherine Gibbs training came in handy, and I filled a much-needed position there as secretary.

The office was bare and antiquated, with no modern equipment. The American Red Cross had certainly spent no money frivolously on it! A single bare bulb hung from the ceiling and provided the only light other than that which came from the windows. The only heat came from a pot-bellied, wood-burning stove. When I complained that the kindling supply was low and that the stove was apt to burn out, the director drawled, "Y'all got to go out and chop some kindlin'." I sat there with my mouth agape, but, if I wanted to be warm, I knew what I must do—and, indeed I did chop the "kindlin'."

This little office in Jacksonville served the entire county in North Carolina in which it stood. It was our responsibility to evaluate a situation for the home office in Washington, DC, when a request for help came in. That meant a good deal of traveling, sometimes at night, and I was frequently asked to accompany the director, who did not like to go out alone. At times when the situation was particularly perilous, we asked Irv, if he were free, to accompany us to give us a feeling of security.

One particular call that I remember clearly reported that a tornado had completely destroyed a nearby small town known as a "black" town, where no whites lived. The three of us climbed into the Red Cross vehicle and drove to the location. It was truly a disaster. Every house but one had been demolished, and they lay collapsed upon themselves along the town's darkened streets. We headed for the remaining house, which, as it turned out, belonged to the minister. As we arrived at the house, we found the minister holding his head, swaying and moaning, "Lord—a—mercy, I thought Judgment Day had come!" We could understand his plight. In the darkness, he warned us to watch where we stepped. We soon found we had trouble keeping our footing as we tried to step over and between the resting but forlorn parishioners to whom he had opened his home on that sad night. They had lost everything! We saw the glass shards of mason jars, which were evidence of even the loss of their canned food supply for the upcoming winter.

We wired Washington that help was definitely needed by this devastated little town. To my amazement, within 24 hours a team arrived from headquarters to evaluate the losses and to calculate the cost of rebuilding. The people were given chits rather than cash to trade for building materials and for food, clothing, and the necessities of life. Our hearts went out to these unfortunate people; we were dismayed, however, that nearby residents, untouched by the tornado, resented the financial help given to this poor town by the American Red Cross!

After a year in Jacksonville, my husband was reassigned and moved on; of course, I went with him, knowing it had been a year I would never forget. Not only did my experience give me an insight into life in a little Southern town, but it also gave me great and lasting respect for the American Red Cross.

With fond memories,
Gerda

*Gerda Woerner (d.1998), a New Jersey native, lived with her architect husband and their son in the Metuchen-Edison area for many years. An excellent swimmer in her youth, she was a candidate for the Olympics at one time. Her professional career was that of legal secretary in a New Brunswick firm.*

# THE NINETEEN FIFTIES

# MY LETTER TO MY GREAT-GRANDCHILDREN-TO-BE

## Felonese Kelley

Dear Great-grandchildren-to-be,

Since my two oldest granddaughters recently married, I am writing to you to tell you a little about myself.

You can figure out that my family and I highly prized education and educational travel. Since I was born in Alabama, my college degree was a Bachelor of Science in pre-med. with a major in chemistry and a minor in biology from Birmingham Southern College. I was admitted to the School of Medicine at the University of Alabama at Tuscaloosa but had to resign after almost a year's residency because of my mother's severe illness. Hence, I had to sell my Piper Cub airplane, my cadaver, my microscope, and my books in order to take care of my mother. Then I taught science at Ensley High School, which was only five blocks away from my parents' home in Birmingham.

After marriage to Joseph Kelley, we moved to many states and then to Metuchen, where I went to Rutgers University and received my Master of Education degree with a major in administration and supervision. Then I became a principal in Woodbridge, where I opened up a new school in 1960, School 23 in Avenel. In

1976, I became principal of School 14 in Fords, from which I retired in January 1986.

During most of this time, my husband and I did a considerable amount of travel throughout the world because he was a chemical engineer and travel was part of his job description.

In 1976, I received my Doctor of Education degree from Fordham University in New York City. So during the recent scandals in Washington, D.C., and with the scandals associated with the Olympics in Salt Lake City, Utah, I took the opportunity to reread my research findings from my dissertation as printed in the *New Jersey School Administrator*, Spring 1997. It made me proud that my paper and research, "Selected Values Clarification Strategies and Elementary School Pupils' Self Concept, School Sentiment and Reading Achievement" were applicable today.

While working on my degree, I was asked to help form policy for a new concept called "Elderhostel." Hence, I have been on as many as 82 Elderhostels all over the world. These colleges and universities that I attended in Elderhostel have taken me to most of the United States, Hawaii, Iceland, Norway, Denmark, England, Scotland, Ireland, Canada, Mexico, Cook Island, French Polynesia, Western Samoa, New Guinea, Easter Island, and Chile. I belong to the Travelers' Century Club, a fact which declares that I have been to over one hundred countries in the world.

One of the most interesting places that I have recently visited was Antarctica, aboard Orient Lines' "Marco Polo" with members of the Grand Circle Travel. One of the high points of the cruise was the opportunity to meet Sir Edmund Hillary, who related his experiences in his historic ascent of Mt. Everest and his tractor expedition to the South Pole. Also traveling with the group and sharing their own unique experiences were: Bradford Washburn, adventurer and former director of Boston's Museum of Science; Barbara Washburn, first woman to climb Mt. McKinley; Leverett Byrd, grandson of Admiral Richard Byrd; Tony Simpson, who related his experiences as a former member of the British Antarctic

Survey Team; and ornithologist Peter Alden, who shared his extensive knowledge of birds.

Leverett spoke about his famous grandfather, Admiral Byrd, and brought along some of the admiral's clothing and personal memorabilia. Also, he gave me a videotape of Admiral Byrd's stay in Antarctica. He had made it from movies of Admiral Byrd when he was in Antarctica. I treasure this tape very highly.

It was a trip that will long be remembered for the spectacular scenery and wild life—the mile-long icebergs floating in a dark sea, the tuxedoed penguins strutting about on rocky shores, the giant seals slumbering in the sun—and for the excitement of setting foot on a land to which few people have traveled. To me it was surreal, like being in a science fiction movie. My sense of perception was absolutely bewildered by the mist, fog, snow, and unreality of it all. I regarded this voyage as a learning experience to interact with and learn from everyone on the trip.

I remember the sights as I looked out my cabin window and saw wonderful ice sculptures in all shapes and forms. I thought that it was an amazing place, frozen in eternity.

One of the high points of the trip was the first zodiac landing at Port Lockroy. After donning heavy clothing, rain suits, parkas, and rubber boots, some of us boarded the zodiacs and, surrounded by petrels, penguins, and albatrosses, rode a mile or so through choppy waters to the landing spot. Once on shore we were treated to the spectacle of thousands of Gentoo penguins, waddling about, stealing rocks from one another, bowing, watching over soon-to-be-hatched eggs. We saw how one mate relieved the other in watching over the nest and how the mate being relieved stood by to make sure that the other did a good job. In addition to the penguins, we saw seals, dolphins, humpback whales, petrels, cormorants, and many other birds during the three-week visit to the world of ice and snow.

The trip ended too soon in Buenos Aires with fine weather and a goodbye dinner, complete with gauchos, slide show of the trip, and fireworks. It was a good voyage that will not be forgotten.

I hope that you, in your lifetime, will attend many colleges and take many educational trips as your Great-grandmother Kelley has done.

Love you,<br>Your Great Grams

*Felonese Kelley, born in Alabama, has lived in Metuchen since 1950. A graduate of Birmingham-Southern College, Rutgers and Fordham Universities, she served Woodbridge School District as principal of two schools for twenty-five years. She has one son, John, and five granddaughters.*

# A FRENCH STREET PERSPECTIVE

## Melody Kokola

Dear Alice,

Well, here is the letter you asked for. It's funny how different our remembrances are because of the six-year difference in our ages, but I can understand your wanting to give your daughters a glimpse of what their "Auntie M" was like as a little girl. And I guess this letter will fill in the blanks for you too.

I started by slowly driving along French Street. You should know that the entire block is different from when we were living there as a bilingual, three-generational family above a neighborhood tavern.

First, the hardware store and Szabo's building are both gone; there is a vacant lot on one side and a hole in the ground on the other. The hole in the ground will become a technical high school for the city of New Brunswick, and my guess is that the curriculum will be health-oriented with possible internships available at Robert Wood Johnson University hospital, just down the block. Do you remember when it was simply called Middlesex Hospital?

The tavern looks so small now that it makes me wonder how it could accommodate all those customers. I remember playing hopscotch and jump rope in the alleyway. It was always cool and shady there. Grandpop used to slowly walk up and down, singing so low under his breath that he seemed to be mumbling. It was only at his death that I learned he was considered by many to be *the* poet of his village in Hungary. He served as everyone's godfather and had a poem for every occasion. I'm sorry I didn't pay more attention to him.

And I remember Grandmom sitting in her chair by the front window—watching comings and goings on French Street. She always seemed to be the "boss" of the family, although "matriarch" sounds so much nicer. Grandpop would frequently sneak a much-folded dollar bill into my hand, and, with a co-conspirator-sounding warning, would tell me not to tell Grandmom.

I guess it was really no surprise, then, to find all those carefully executed legal documents after her death, detailing numerous loans made to and repaid by people who emigrated after the 1956 uprising. And I remember her anger at the loss of family acreage to the Russian Communists, land she had helped purchase.

I remember walking with Grandpop around the corner and down to the Middlesex County Court House—the old one with the magnificent columns—which was replaced by a cold, sterile-looking, rectangle of a building. There was a coffee shop in the basement, and we would stop and get a small glass bottle of milk and share it while sitting on a bench in the shade. Then we'd walk home.

Oh, and I remember shopping on French Street: at the meat market and produce market across the street, at the hardware store next door, and at the bakery down the block. This was also a time when you could send a child to the store and not worry about her getting home safely. How times have changed. I also remember being sent to the "chicken lady" around the corner and returning with a brown-paper wrapped package. Everything was within walking distance: Washington School, Tomkins Ice Cream Parlor, the bank, and church. And oh, the shopping on George Street before the era of the malls!

I remember delivering beer and soda with Daddy in the green Buick. I would sit on the cases in the back seat for a better view. And I remember standing on the front seat when I was even younger —no seat belt in place, only an adult arm holding me upright as we came to a stop.

You probably remember doing homework with Mom. Were you ever able to quickly add the column of numbers in your head the way she did—and still does? I never was. And although I always expected to attend college, I recently learned with some surprise that Grandmom thought it would be a wasteful expense because after all, I would "only" get married. I owe more to Mom than I ever could repay.

So this is just a bit of "little" me. I'll have to put on my thinking cap for more stories for the girls. Take care, and kiss everyone for me.

Love,
Melody

*Melody Kokola was born in New Brunswick and has lived in New Jersey her entire life. She graduated from Douglass College and Columbia University, has been a librarian for 22 years, and has served as Director of the Metuchen Public Library since 1986. A mother of two adult children, she worked for the Edison Post Office as its first female carrier during her college summers and still owns her first new car—a '68 GTO.*

# DRESS REHEARSAL

## Mary Ellen Malague

Dear Rose, Peg, Marty, and Kate,

When we were all together last month for our fortieth wedding anniversary celebration, I was recalling a story that you urged me to write in all its details. Remember, this is my version of the story!

I'll begin with that memorable occasion of the crowning of the statue of the Blessed Mother, an event taking place in St. James Church in Woodbridge on a beautiful day in May. In those days of the fifties and earlier, the traditional crowning was repeated year after year in almost every Catholic church. In 1956 it was my turn to assume the role of "crowner." So much tradition and planning had gone into the event . . . even more than I had realized at that time!

Our special group in the church was called the "Young Ladies Sodality," a social and spiritual group for unmarried women in the eighteen and over range. Today's "singles" groups are similar but co-ed and probably more honest about their goals. I don't think ours was ever intended to be a match-making group, but it had that sort of undertone, considering we spent just as much time talking about how to meet boyfriends as how to pray or how to abide by Catholic doctrines. While retreats, speakers, and charity work were always on the agenda, the main events of the year—what might be called the hidden agenda—seemed to be the farewell parties in the form of bridal showers for the marrying members . . . and, of course, the May crowning, each year's culminating event. A few of the Sisters of Mercy from St. James Convent enjoyed their roles as advisers for the group; their mission was probably to recruit likely candidates for their community, but, while they occasionally were successful in that, they were also known to join in the efforts to promote matches of couples in the parish.

Each year in May, the president of this group led a procession along the street and into the church, and, with great ceremony, she reverently placed a crown of lovely lilies of the valley upon the brilliantly painted statue of Mary. The other young ladies, dressed in blue or white gowns, were accompanied by darling little girls decked out with puffy white dresses and flower-laden baskets. The four or five-year-old crown bearer, traditionally a little boy, usually stole the show. The singular distinction of wearing a bridal gown and veil belonged to the crowner.

And so, in 1956, it was my turn to be in this particular spotlight. Feeling blessed by such an honor, I went to daily Mass and tried to prepare myself spiritually, but I quickly got entangled in all the other preparations. My mother, who always was a very involved participant in my activities, accompanied me to Goerke's, a pleasant department store in the old and elegant Elizabeth, NJ, as I looked for a bargain on the bridal dress rack. Suiting me best was a quite beautiful gown—lace, silk, net, etc.—and a cleaning was all it needed to get rid of its "sample" status. While I swirled in front of the mirror in the dressing room, the train flowed and the veil shimmered, and my mother and I were delighted.

Yes, the day was absolutely perfect for this spectacular event. (You have seen the pictures.) The scene was set with lots of flowers, ushers, a Knights of Columbus procession, a packed church, a woman in bridal attire, and her attendants: everything needed for a wedding but a groom! Little did I know that one of the nuns was busy providing one that evening!

Now it is important that you understand that Sister Rose Mary was one of the Sister of Mercy-advisers at the time of my crowning. As the story has been told and retold, she had selected me several years before as a possible mate for her brother, who was living in Belleville but working in the old Woodbridge RCA plant.

Without any knowledge on my part, her plotting and planning had reached the status of a joke in the convent, even among those sisters who had given up in their consideration of me as a candidate to join them.

Well, after the crowning ceremony, which was, in my opinion, the best ever, our family followed the tradition of providing light refreshments at a reception in the parish hall to greet all the attendees. And there he was! The brother and his mother had been dragged all the way from Belleville to Woodbridge for this important meeting, some three years in the planning. As a non-participant in this plot, I was unaware of its significance; I smiled, greeted, and moved on.

You might say the rest is history. But not quite. Three years later and many trips between Belleville and Woodbridge ensued before we decided that the Sisters were, indeed, good matchmakers! And so, a real wedding was planned.

I think you knew your Grandma well enough to understand that this mother of mine would once again be a central figure in arranging an important event in my life. This time, however, we didn't take a trip to a bridal shop in pursuit of the perfect new wedding dress. No. "No need to buy another dress when you have a perfectly good one in the attic!" she said, in her endearing, ever-practical way. So up we went up to the attic to shake out the once-worn Goerke bridal dress. In a mood more practical than obedient or sentimental, I tried it on, had to inhale a few pounds that had been added, and agreed, in the words of a child of the Depression, that "It will do." I also knew quite well that my mother, who loved things elegant and perfect, would not lead me astray.

And so it was on a beautiful day in June 1959, in the very same St. James Church in Woodbridge, that my dress and I reappeared. The attendants were fewer, but the church was again flower-filled and packed with family, neighbors, friends, and students. My dress, none the worse for wear, as the expression goes, elegantly moved with me down the aisle to meet the addition to this event, the groom—Aunt Rose Mary's brother, your father! I don't think anyone noticed the dress was the same, and I didn't tell.

So that's the story! Whoever said it isn't good luck to see the bride in her bridal dress before the wedding probably did not mean three years before. Do you think I might be the only person ever to meet her husband under such circumstances? As for bad luck . . . so far we have had forty fulfilling, lovely years. And the dress? It was tossed out long ago, never recovering from the strain of the second wearing. I am sorry it is not available for my daughters and granddaughters, but, after all, it had done its job.

With all my love,
Mom

*Mary Ellen Malague was born in Woodbridge and lived in the Metuchen area for 34 years until her move to the New Jersey Shore. A graduate of Douglass College and Rutgers University, she has had careers as mother of four, teacher in the Woodbridge School District, and Director of the Milltown and Cranbury Libraries. She joined the club in 1987 and currently serves as president.*

# THE NINETEEN SIXTIES

# READ THIS WHEN YOU'RE ALL GROWN UP

## Rev. Barbara C. Crafton

Dear Madeline,

It is not my expectation that you will read this until you are older. I don't know if you've read my other books—pieces of them, I guess, the parts that are about you. I can't think you'd seek out a book by the Quiet Hour Club—at least, not yet.

But you might when you're older. Specifically, you might when I have died, and you and your sister and your mommy and your aunt are going through my things. I wanted to read everything my parents left lying around. I hungered for their presence in between the lines. I saved letters, sermons, recipes, even checkbook registers for a while. We read the words of the beloved dead in great thirsty gulps, hoping somehow to find again the feeling of them alive. And sometimes we do find a lick of it here and there: a snatch of presence, the sudden scent of a long-ago perfume, a few bars of a forgotten song. We go looking for these things amid the forest of their written words, and we usually find a few scraps.

What I'm going to leave lying around in this letter is important. If I sat you down and told you, you'd be embarrassed, and I don't want to embarrass you. But I do want you to know.

When I was four, I embarrassed my mother by proclaiming to our maid, "Marjorie, you're chocolate and we're vanilla."

When I was five, I found my mother crying in front of the television set. I had never seen her cry before. She was watching a little girl walking on her way to school. The street along which she walked was lined with adults: they were coming out at her from the crowd, coming too close, shouting at her, shaking their fists, and twisting their faces. "What are they doing?" I asked. She turned off the set and went upstairs.

In those days in that place, we had drinking fountains labeled "Whites Only" and "Colored." We had separate rest rooms and separate motels; theirs were called "Colored Cabins." A place out on Route 1 kept that sign up well into the 1970s. You never saw a black person eating in a restaurant. I don't think I ever saw one shopping for clothing.

One day on the television I saw the governor of Georgia standing in the door of a school. I saw three or four young people sit at a soda fountain, and I saw a large white man behind the counter, paralyzed, not knowing what to do.

I also saw Amos n' Andy on the television; one Christmas, Amos bought his little girl a sled, even though they lived in a city with no hills and there was no snow. I saw him and his wife put their little one to bed on Christmas Eve, look at her for a moment, and then tiptoe from the room. The last frame was her bedroom window—snow began to fall over the roofs of the apartment buildings outside.

In the third grade, our teacher had something important to say to us on the last day of school. "Colored children are going to come to school here next year," she said. "They have to. We have to let them." Her face was without expression. But no colored children came in fourth grade. Or in fifth. Neither did they come the next year. And then I went to the next town, to junior high school.

Yardley, the company that made my grandmother's lavender cologne, also had a fragrance called "Bond Street." In town, the colored people's neighborhood ran along Bond Street. Kids used to see that cologne in the drug store. "Oh, why don't you buy some Bond Street?" they'd say, and they would laugh.

Berta Mae Bailey was in my seventh grade class. She was dark and smart and guarded. Another girl put her hand on Berta's arm once. "Quit!" Berta said, and jerked her arm away. On her notebook, where we used to write boys' names and titles of favorite records, she wrote the name of her old school.

Ann Ryan dated a black basketball player in ninth grade; he was older. Jane Duiguid dated a black boy. They were the only two. Ann's parents sent her to boarding school the next year. Jane stayed and didn't date anybody after that. After high school, Mike Norris dated a black girl whose name I don't recall. But I remember that she was smart. Mike had been president of the student council.

One summer, a village of tents sprang up on the Mall in Washington, D.C. It was called Resurrection City. It was a city of black people. I went there to talk to them. I thought I might write a story about it for the local newspaper. I sat down on the ground beside a young woman. Could I ask her some questions? "Should I talk to her?" she asked a young man nearby. He looked at me indifferently and shrugged. I felt foolish. I stammered out a few silly questions. "What is Watts like?" and got monosyllabic responses. I never wrote the story.

Martin Luther King had been shot during the night. I found out about it when I woke up. On television people were burning buildings and getting shot. A man walked by carrying an enormous television set. The coffin traveled along in a wagon drawn by mules. Silent black people lined the route, tears streaming down their faces.

Some people at the university had signs in their windows that read "Angela Davis is Welcome Here." She had been a college professor; now she was a fugitive, sought by the FBI in connection with a terrorist incident.

Two victorious Olympic athletes raised their fists in the Black Power salute during the playing of the American national anthem. People thought it was a disgrace. For fifty years there had been a song known as the "Negro National Anthem." I had never heard it. Didn't know there was such a thing.

I had a lunch with one of my college professors just before I started seminary. We stood by my car in the parking lot afterward while I rummaged for my keys; he was waiting with me until I got safely inside. A white man saw us standing together and thought we were a couple. He shot us a hateful look and spat on the ground.

Your sister has a head of curly light brown hair. Your hair is shiny and black. Her skin is pale. Yours is the color of café au lait. Her eyes are light brown. Your eyes flash black, your eyelashes long and beautiful. The mother of one of Rosie's friends told her daughter that you must have had different fathers because you look so different. You have the same father. I wanted to find that mother and tell her that. I wanted to tell her that some things are none of her business. I wanted to tell her that she needed something with which to occupy her mind more profitably. If she had one. I wanted to shame the bejesus out of her.

But I didn't want you to know. I don't want you to know any of these things. Not until you're old enough.

                With love and admiration for who you are,
                Mamo

*Barbara Cawthorne Crafton, the daughter and sister of Episcopalian priests, is a graduate of the New York General Theological Seminary. Currently the Rector of St. Clemens Episcopal Church of New York City, she previously served as curate of St. Luke's Episcopal Church of Metuchen and as Director of the Seafarers' Services at Seamen's Church Institute of New York and New Jersey. Author, vocalist, dramatist, and director, she is the mother of two daughters and grandmother of two granddaughters.*

# TYROLEAN POLENTA PARTIES

## Carol Cuneo

Dearest Nonna Emma,

I am writing to you, regretfully, at a time when it is much too late in my life, a time after you have left your life in this world; but I believe that you truly will receive this message through heavenly, angelic messengers.

We had never met while you were in this world, and I arrived after your death at age 34, so there is a bit of catching up to do. I hope you are peaceful up there in heaven and this will prepare us to meet someday.

We have, from what little I was told about you, some traits in common: We are both petite, are housewives, have siblings, and are from the Baldessari family. Did you know we are from royalty? Baldessari is a name derived from "Baldes," a Germanic pet form of the name "Balthasar," who was one of the three kings.

Our similarity ends at that point. You bore seven children, I none. In fact, your sixth child, Wilbert Baldessari, is my father. Your daughters Josephine and Rina have told me Willie is much like your husband, Vincento Baldessari. Both had crusty, dry hands from manual labor; yet, both possessed sensitive, bruised souls that they soothed with alcohol. (Isn't it sad for men? They do not know any other way to take the rigors of a hard life.)

Recently, at age eighty-six, Aunt Rina decided to share some letters and communications between Grandpa Vincento, who had made his way to Ellis Island, and his sisters, who had stayed behind in Europe. One letter, surprisingly written in Italian, thanked Vincent profusely for the $2.00 he had mailed to them after their village had been destroyed by bombs in WWII. I was so surprised to learn there were still relatives in Europe, as Willie never spoke about it. I find it very interesting that you and Grandpa did speak and write in Italian, even though you emigrated from a part of Austria called the Tyrol. As a coal miner in Pennsylvania, Grampa Vincento must have worked desperately to keep a roof over your poverty-stricken heads. I call myself the "coal miner's granddaughter." Even though he never spoke of his young life very much, Willie must have secretly wanted to keep some of his childhood memories alive. For many years during the 1960s, he and his wife Evie (my mother) would hold the family reunion picnic right at our suburban home in South Plainfield, New Jersey.

The yearly reunion was the single most exciting event of the year for me and for my older brother Jim and my baby sister Suzie. We are all proud of the Tyrolean descent we inherited from you both, and at this particular family gathering, we ate traditional foods that were introduced here by Tyroleans and Italians alike. The one staple, we learned, on which the Baldessari children survived in Pennsylvania, was cornmeal mush, better know as polenta (now a gourmet delicacy served in many fine restaurants). In fact, the reunion was dubbed "The Polenta Party" by the family members, and now even thirty years later, my cousins still recount fond memories from Uncle Willie's Polenta Parties.

When the time was right, Willie would quickly and skillfully cook the polenta in a large pot, mold it onto a large platter, and dance around the yard to blaring music, holding the steaming platter high over his head as if it were the prized catch of the day. Everyone would cheer, and the ceremonial serving would commence. The bland tasting, yellow, grainy-textured food was definitely something one had to acquire a taste for over time. I was always willing to try anything, but polenta was hard to take unless it was smothered with the accompanying veal stew and served with a side dish of marinated peas and a dessert of shoo-fly pie. I could just picture you in your long-sleeved dress as a young mother, holding a baby in one arm and stirring the copper polenta pot over a coal stove with the other.

The Polenta Party offered us a chance to acquaint ourselves with some relatives who didn't visit often and who brought some of the old country ways with them. Uncle Tommy always arrived equipped with his plastic container of escargots (snails . . . yuk!!!!) Do you know he would sit down and slurp those things into his mouth one by one!? I ran away fast when he offered me some samples. Later, I saw him strolling around the yard picking tiny dandelion leaves and munching them on the spot.

I never knew anyone as old as your sister Mary, who was 75. I was afraid of her and would peer at her across the living room in her black dress, which, we understand, she wore all year round; her voice and hands would pulse with palsy when she would speak with a sing-song kind of brogue. I was fascinated by my numerous older cousins, who all had big smiling faces and loud voices. Isn't it funny that we Tyroleans have such large voices, yet are known for being diminutive? Aunt Rina, who is 4' 8" tall, clipped an advertisement out of the newspaper at Christmas time. It was for an artificial tree which the company called a "Tyrolean" tree, but she couldn't figure out what made it Tyrolean. When I read the ad, it said the trees were 4' 5" tall. "That's the Tyrolean part," I said. "They're small trees." Everyone roared laughing in their big voices.

The thing that made me feel most filled up at the reunions was not really the food. Food for the soul is more what I liked. At these reunions I wish you could have been here to sing along in your sweet voice while I played the guitar and my brother played the accordion. Everyone else loved us to pieces when we played music. In pure Tyrolean fashion, they yodeled all the old tunes to our music and stuffed our pockets with dollar bills. This was good training: I have served my church for thirty years now as a music minister, song leader, and soloist.

Nonna Emma, before I close this letter, I want to thank you for bringing life into this world, for in doing so you brought me to life. I learned that many of the things I enjoy most had been enjoyed by your children, and so I assume that means you also enjoyed them. And when I think of that, I believe that I may know you a little bit, even though I have never met you.

      Love,
      Your Little Granddaughter Carol Baldessari-Cuneo

*Carol Cuneo, a resident of Middlesex County for 45 years, and married to Raymond Cuneo Jr. for 17 years, earned a BS from Rutgers University and an MA in Communications from Fairleigh Dickinson University. Employed as a soloist for Sacred Heart Roman Catholic Church in South Plainfield, Carol is a cantor for the Rutgers Catholic Campus Ministry. Prior to that she was a food technologist with General Foods Corporation.*

# THE CANASTA GAME

## Bette Daniele

Dear Daughter,

I had a happy, normal, and boring childhood. As I look back, I cannot recall any defining moments that shaped my character forever. Unlike the protagonists of literature, I cannot point to one event and say, "Yes! That is the moment when I grew up." A normal childhood. However, I do remember the first time my siblings and I were invited to join the world of adults. It wasn't a wedding, a funeral, or other event normally associated with the passage into adulthood. It was a card game.

Is there anyone of my generation who didn't play canasta as a child? A recent episode of "The Nanny," of all things, brought back a flood of memories of THE CARD GAME.

My mother and her friends played bridge. There were duplicate games with dinner on Saturday nights; Monday nights were reserved for the "girls." As a child growing up in the sixties, I associated bridge with hats, gloves, and pastel colored mints, none of which I particularly liked. Bridge was boring beyond belief. None of my sisters nor I ever learned to play. However, we all learned to play canasta. You see, Bridge, with a capital B, was played in the living room. Canasta, however, was a kitchen table sort of game. Whereas bridge went with the aforementioned mints, canasta went with potato chips and soda.

My grandmother and all her friends played canasta. Learning to play canasta with my grandmother was a rite of passage in my family. My grandmother taught us to play on Saturday night sleepovers at her house. Sitting at her kitchen table, she patiently explained the nuances of melding, the counting of points, and the differences between canastas with jokers and those without. We started playing two-handed only, which always resulted in some crazy scores, before she added first one sister and then the other to the mix. We had arrived at partnership canasta!

Of course, once my grandmother taught us, we were off and running. At the pool, on rainy days, and on sleepovers with friends (all of whom also seemed to have learned from their grandparents), we refined our skills. We were convinced we were canasta mavens. Little did we know that my grandmother was honing our skills for bigger and better things.

The big moment came when we were down the shore. Every summer we rented a house at the beach, and every summer my grandmother would spend the month of August with us, playing cards with us at night and visiting with her cousins during the days. Her cousins, also known as the "girls from Rahway," although none of them was a day younger than 55, were the nieces and nephews of her deceased husband. They were somewhat exotic ladies to us, mostly because of their odd names and lack of children. There were Al, Edge, Jon, and Maud, all of whom I learned years later did have real names; to wit, Alice, Edna, Helen, and Maud. They were card buffs all.

And so it came to pass that on one stormy night we were all invited to join the adult canasta game. I remember sitting around the table in our dark and damp bungalow, with the black and white portable TV in the corner feebly trying to transmit the Yankees' game. There were, I am sure, pretzels and bridge mix. We girls drank soda; the "girls" and my grandmother were politely sipping on their nips—those little seven ounce bottles of beer that my grandmother and her friends liked—because they could never finish more beer than that.

We girls were all quiet and concentrating mightily; after all, we had been partnered with the "girls from Rahway." Woe be it to any of us if we incorrectly counted our points for a meld or picked up the pot when it was too big or too small. For the first hand or so, we held back, following our partners' leads.

But then each of us got her sea legs. A bad pun, I know, but we were down the shore. After all, the Queen of the Canasta Players, my grandmother, had taught us the game. I am sure that in later life we all have done things that have made her proud, but in this instance she was glowing. After all, her talented and brainy grandchildren were excelling at something that she had taught us! As for us, we didn't talk much, preferring to listen to the adult gossip. Oh, did we feel worldly!

I know we played with the cousins in later summers, until the allure of the boardwalk became too great, and sitting with the grown-ups no longer appealed. Been there, done that. We never played much after that. I have tried to play in later years, but everyone I meet has a different set of rules for the game, much like trying to play Monopoly. But, interestingly enough, mention canasta, and almost everyone immediately remembers grandparents or an elderly aunt who taught them the game.

Love,<br>Mom

*Bette Daniele is a life-long resident of the area. A graduate of the College of William and Mary, she is a Certified Public Accountant and Accredited Personal Financial Specialist. She lives in Edison with her husband and daughter.*

# THE NINETEEN SEVENTIES

# EUROPE BY CAMPER

## Roberta Ambler

Dear Bobbi, Nancy, and David,

Recently, at the dinner table we were asked, "What was your favorite trip ever?" Dad hesitated, saying, "Different ones for different reasons." I thought the same, but then said, "Our family camping trip in Europe." And I will stick to that thought! But I have wondered since what the three of you remember, whether your memories are the same as ours and how much my own memories are colored by having recently reviewed my slides of the trip.

It was a great idea Dad had: to take the three of you out of school for three weeks and to rent a camper and just drive around. (The few Europeans we met were aghast at the idea of a holiday from school.) Our itinerary was formed by studying library books and *Europe on $5 a Day*, by remembering places we had read about years ago, and by trying to adapt to your ages, 16, 14, and 10; so we went light on museums.

I remember our first foray to the campground supermarket in Holland, where we could not find eggs until Dad acted out the hen laying an egg. He still loves to tell that story. We soon felt at home in our rented VW camper. It was provided with a minimum of dishes and cookware. There were a camp stove and a small refrigerator and a sort of tent which sheltered our eating area. We, who had always used many paper cups on our other camping trips, found that we could manage with the five furnished cups, each a different color. We soon set out to explore Amsterdam, where I remember the canals, the cobblestone streets, and the people dressed in business clothes riding their bicycles to work. The time was May, and the array of tulips spread out in the Keukenhof gardens remains a colorful memory. We went to Marken in order to look for the traditional scenes that Dad and I remembered from the *National Geographic* magazines of our youth. We saw only a few people in traditional costumes with wooden shoes, and we had to drive to a different town to find windmills.

Belgium is a blur in my memory because we drove straight across the country to get to France. I am sorry now that we did not take a day to visit some of the quaint Belgian cities.

We somehow crossed the border into France without finding a money-changer, so we had to detour to a small city, Arras, to find a bank. There was a bonus—an open-air market in the town square. Colorful banners flapped overhead in contrast to the old surrounding buildings, and there were booths selling clothing and food of all sorts. In Paris we found the recommended campground in the Bois de Boulogne, under horse chestnut trees on the banks of the Seine. We laughed about the young man who set up a folding lawn chair outside the fence to admire our "beautiful daughter," driving her inside in embarrassment. Our bus tour of Paris by night told us that it was V-E Day, with special lighting and flags on l'Arc de Triomphe. On other days we rode the Metro to do normal tourist things. Dad and I remember walking down the Champs Elysee behind you two leggy girls and watching two young men try to pick you up. I think you were glad Dad was nearby.

I know we all remember the visit to the family of Nancy's penpal when I struggled to communicate with her father. The two penpals and their older sisters were all too shy to talk much. You girls tasted your first champagne. And there was an older brother who rode each of you around on his motor scooter.

Leaving Paris, we had views of pastoral country and tree-lined lanes as we headed for Normandy. Mont St. Michel was our first attraction. We parked our camper on the shore and walked out the causeway toward the island in the twilight, drawn toward it by a mysterious attraction. Exploring it the next day was equally fascinating. Then it was on to Rouen because Bobbi was doing a paper on Joan of Arc for school. We saw the wax museum's depiction of Joan's trial and death and visited the lovely cathedral nearby. We circled around Paris to the Loire Valley and from there straight east to Switzerland. There was a lovely isolated campground in the eastern mountains where the air was fresh and bracing, and the cows coming down to be milked passed by our camper with a tinkle of bells.

The Swiss Alps were as breathtakingly beautiful as we had always dreamed they would be. We enjoyed fondue, both the cheese and beef varieties, and hearty soups. We camped in a meadow near a fine thread of a waterfall with mountains all around. We traveled by a series of cable cars up the Schildhorn to view the Jungfrau from the revolving restaurant at the top. Another day we found our way up a steep, winding road to the Girl Scouts' "Our Chalet," so we three Girl Scouts could say that we had been there. How disappointing to find it closed! David decided he would walk down rather than experience that road again in the camper. One morning in Zurich, we wakened to a holiday with all the banks and food stores closed. We lunched at a lakeside restaurant which would take our American Travelers' Checks. I asked the waiter what kind of holiday it was. He replied, "I do not know. I am Hongary." (It was Ascension Day.)

We had been told that after Switzerland, everything would be downhill during our return journey. And so it was, geographically and emotionally. There are no strong memories of the rest of the trip. We visited cathedrals in Strasbourg and Cologne, rode along the Rhine, and re-entered Holland near the town of Arnhem. There we had a fun visit to a drive-through animal park. The ostriches looked as if they were acting as ticket-takers.

The thing that made this trip so special to me was that it was a first trip to Europe for all five of us, a time of sharing. There are many other places I wish we had seen, but we tried to consider your ages and interests. Anyway, it was fun, wasn't it?

Love,<br>
Mom

*Roberta Ambler was born and lived all her life in Middlesex County until her move to Bridgewater three years ago. She graduated from Douglass College and worked for eleven years as a research chemist for General Foods Corporation before retiring to raise her three children. She is a past president of the Quiet Hour Club.*

# ON WINGS OF JOY

## Alberta Bachman

Dear Kaila, Amy, and Marielle,

Although you are still very young and at this time perhaps not too interested in your ancestral history, I am hoping that twenty or thirty years from now you might wonder a little about your Gramdmom's lifestyle. Many exciting events have taken place over the years, but one in particular that you might enjoy knowing about was the time I took my first solo flight. I had begun taking flying lessons at age 46 after your Grandpop and I had taken a Discovery Flight. We had enjoyed the experience so much that we decided to pursue our interest in flying.

On April 18, 1978, I was introduced to Scott, a 24-year-old-man who would be my flight instructor for the next few months. He turned out to be a very patient person who instilled a lot of confidence in his students, especially me. He taught me to "feel" the aircraft I was flying so it became a part of me. His instruction included all kinds of flight maneuvers, flight rules, ground rules, instrument readings, radio communications, weather knowledge–everything that was necessary for me to become a safe pilot. We flew to airports all over New Jersey, New York, and Pennsylvania with me at the controls and Scott in the right seat, making sure that I was doing everything right. After weeks of cross-country flights and hundreds of take-offs and landings, I felt quite confident that I was ready to handle the aircraft all by myself. Whenever I asked Scott about this, he was non-committal and would usually respond, "Pretty soon" or "One of these days." Well, to me, "pretty soon" was not soon enough, and I was becoming a little frustrated. I wanted to solo!

One morning I had a flight lesson scheduled very early—8:30. Although the weather was a little overcast and the commuter traffic on the highway very heavy, I managed to arrive at the airport at the appointed time. My instructor, however, was nowhere in sight. After patiently waiting for him for one and a half hours (I read every magazine in the flight office!), he finally called and said he would be a little late. At this point, I was furious! As a person who always keeps appointments and is never late for anything, I have very little patience for people who don't respect other people's schedules.

Finally, at 11:00 AM, Scott arrived, all smiling and apologetic, explaining that the earlier weather conditions wouldn't have been too good for flying anyway! I coolly dismissed his banter and went outside to do my preflight for the aircraft. I guess I was emotionally still steaming because when we were in the air, Scott didn't say too much while I was going through my various flight maneuvers. His only comments were: "That's good," "Do those 60 degree accelerated banks and turns again," and "Try some more of those stalls." No friendly small talk, just all serious business.

When our lesson time was over, I landed the airplane. As I was quietly taxiing back to the airport, Scott jumped down from the plane and said, "Okay, take it up!" "Excuse me," I said, "you mean ALONE?" "Of course," he replied, "after this morning, you're more than ready!!" I guess all the anger and frustration from the early hours forced the adrenaline to pump overtime and helped me to display my abilities to fly that plane and convince Scott that I could fly by myself!

Now that the time had actually arrived for me to solo the aircraft, I became very apprehensive, and reality set in! I had to perform perfectly all alone—there was no one to help me and no room for mistakes.

As I slowly taxied to the runway, my confidence kicked in again as I realized that I had to prove myself proficient if I wanted to come down safely. I approached the runway, said a little prayer, and pushed the throttle. I gained speed rapidly and lifted off the ground faster than I ever had before when Scott was in the seat beside me. He warned me about this beforehand, explaining that there would be less weight and drag to contend with.

Once I was airborne, exhilaration took over: "This is the greatest and I'm doing it all by myself!" I accelerated up to 1200 feet to get into the flight pattern, flew downwind, then base, then the final approach to land the plane safely on the runway. What a great feeling! As I taxied back to the airport terminal, Scott was there smiling and giving me the thumbs up with instructions to take the plane up twice more. I felt wonderful!

On the third time around, however, an unexpected occurrence took place. It began to rain. Now an airplane differs from an automobile insofar as there are no windshield wipers! Luckily, the speed of the airborne aircraft causes the rain to flow off somewhat, but it still is disconcerting to the pilot!

I knew I had no choice but to land the plane safely—and so I did, but not without some trepidation. When I finally exited the plane, I actually felt giddy, but relieved. Scott was there to congratulate and hug me and assure me that I had done a great job in spite of the adverse conditions. We continued into the terminal, where he proceeded to cut off the bottom back of my T-shirt and print the words with a magic marker:

Alberta Bachman<br>
1<sup>st</sup> Solo Flight<br>
9/8/78

I was ecstatic!! Even though I was on the ground, I was still flying high.

Several more months of flying instruction and cross-country flights with Scott took place, but many of the practice flights and cross-country flights to other airports were done alone. Then came the FAA written examination, followed by a test flight with a certified FAA flight inspector and, finally, my bona fide Private Pilot license. What a thrill!

This was the beginning of many more wonderful years of happy flying to explore new heights and soar with the eagles!

Well, my wonderful granddaughters, I trust you enjoyed this letter. Perhaps while reading, you were even able to vicariously experience the thrill of flying!! I sincerely hope that when you are old enough, you too might have the desire and the opportunity to learn to fly. Then you will know and see what "a little closer to heaven" means.

Love and hugs,<br>Grandmom

*Alberta Bachman, a native New Jerseyan, graduated from Douglass College with a degree in Music Education. After teaching in the public school system, she concentrated on her role as Organist/Choir Director in several churches. A mother of four and grandmother of four, she holds a Private Pilot's License and currently lives in Knoxville, Tennessee, with her husband Don.*

# BRINGING UP PARENTS

## Ellen Donahay

My dear Kristie,
   While I am waiting for your Dad to wake up from a well-deserved nap, I thought I would write another reminiscence of my life to add to those that you and Nancy have been prodding me to record. Let's call this one "The BEST of My Experiences in Education."
   You've often heard me say that the most rewarding part of my non-teaching duties as Supervisor of Home Economics was curriculum development. It was so challenging to design courses for high school students that would not only interest them, but would also help them live happy, meaningful, and productive adult lives. I had chaired many curriculum committees, but I don't think I have to tell you which of all the courses we developed was my pride and joy. Designing and then teaching "Education for Parenthood," with its "Child Development Learning Laboratory" component, was taking a step in education that I felt was long overdue. It was a pioneer program for New Jersey in which our school and only two others participated. The following quote from Edward Zigler, Former Director of the Office of Child Development, Cornell University, crystallized my philosophy of child-rearing and encouraged me to move forward: "I have long believed that the development of a child does not begin the day he/she is born—or at age three—but much earlier, during the formative years of her/his parents."
   After studying human behavior with emphasis on the influences of heredity and environment, the human emotions, human

needs, and mental mechanisms, the students learned the growth and development characteristics of the young child. In November, we brought eighteen four-year-olds into our playschool. The students took turns working with the children in various activities.

Observing the teens working with the children was such a delight for me. I can relive some of those precious moments as though they were just happening. I can still see Allison, children circled around her, reading with such expression and animation that her audience was mesmerized. We all grew in our story-reading skills as we listened to Allison.

Then there was the day when a little girl, complete with apron and utensils, was busy in the child's kitchen cooking dinner. Her "husband," carrying a stack of papers, came home from work. The greeting from the "wife" was priceless. She said, "Oh hello, honey. Sit down and have a cocktail; the skettie's almost ready."

There was one little girl named Susie who was an absolute doll, and her mother dressed her like one. She had curly, flaxen hair and large, bright blue eyes that glistened when she smiled, which was very often. One day I observed Susie working with finger paints and without a smock to protect her dress. I said, "Suzy, please ask Miss Joan to put a smock on you." She replied with a smile and a wave of her hand, "Don't worry, Mrs. Donahay; Mommie will SHOUT it out." How I wished we had been videotaping at that moment! It would have been a perfect commercial for the laundry detergent, SHOUT.

And then there was Eddie, who spent half of his time hiding under the tables. He participated only when he would be working alone, but if it were a group activity, under the table he would go. The students never stopped trying to coax him out to join his classmates. One day in the spring, we all took a walk around the outside of the school. The lawn was speckled with bright yellow dandelions, and Eddie picked a bouquet for me. I thanked him and praised him for being so thoughtful. "Why don't you pick some for Mommie?" I encouraged. He started to walk on the lawn to get more when I called out to the children, "Let's all pick some of the pretty flowers." They responded immediately, running in all directions onto the lawn. Eddie stopped in his tracks, turned around, and returned to my side. If everyone were going to do it, he was going to stop.

The students would discuss Eddie in class and tried one technique after another to lure him out of his table hide-away. Just two days before our graduation ceremonies marking the end of playschool, we were playing a game called "Duck, Duck, Goose." One of the students patiently tried to get Eddie to join the others. To our astonishment, Eddie slowly walked to the circle of children and waited to be tapped. I was so overwhelmed that tears welled up and spilled freely down my face. As I wiped them away, I looked at the students and didn't see one dry eye. The child who was the tapper seemed to sense what was happening, and, as if he had been coached, he circled the children, saying "Duck, duck, duck, duck," and when he reached Eddie, he shouted, "GOOSE!" as he tapped his head.

It was rewarding experiences like these that helped the students learn so much about children. They learned what four-year-olds could and could not be expected to do. They learned about individual differences and how to encourage, to make them feel secure, to help them without taking over their task. They learned what behavior on their part brought desirable responses from the children. The teens grew side by side with the children. How much better can it get?

Our program became one of the models in the state, and many teachers came to observe. I was privileged, with the help of two of our teachers, to write a state curriculum guide for the course. This was followed by a narrated slide presentation we developed entitled "Bringing Up Parents," which was used as a vehicle to convince Boards of Education, school administrators, and parent groups of the value of such a program.

Why was this the "best" of my career? Because I have always been concerned with helping young people become more mature adults—ready to assume the tasks that they will meet in life, especially that of parenting. Like the ever-widening rings a stone makes when dropped into the water, good parenting has an effect on children which will affect their children, which will affect their children—producing circles of influence that could reach shores of potential we can only imagine.

I hope this reminiscence is not too long for your collection, but you know how I go on about my never-to-be-forgotten little ones. And by the way, a great big "thank you" to you and Nancy for the eight precious ones that I don't have to say goodbye to on graduation day! Write soon.

Love,<br>Mother

*Ellen Donahay was born of Danish immigrant parents in Tottenville, Staten Island. A graduate of Douglass College and Rutgers University, her careers have included the raising of two daughters, working as the Technical Assistant to the Director of Research for a chemical firm and as teacher and then supervisor of home economics for the public schools of Edison Township.*

# PIQUE-NIQUE

## Audray Noyes

Dear Mom and Dad,

It has been a while since I wrote, but, as you can imagine, life here has been so very busy. I know I have written so much about our experiences here in Auvergne (really the heart of France), but there is always more to tell you.

A few weeks ago, one of our neighbors rang our bell to invite us for drinks Sunday afternoon. When we got there, the group was excitedly discussing the possibility of having a neighborhood picnic. Since this is a fairly new block with only six houses, this had not been done before. When would we have it? Should we have it? Where would we have it? The "debate" went on for the rest of the afternoon. The group finally decided that we would certainly need another afternoon to devote more time to the most important aspect of all—the menu. A date was made for drinks the next Sunday. When that day arrived, the group reconvened. This time the discussion was even more animated. "We must have grilled sardines," said Mr. Coudert. "Oh yes," the others answered and went on with the menu. Sausages, pâtés, breads, cornichons, tabbouleh, salads, desserts, wines were all considered picnic fare. "Don't forget the sardines," repeated Mr. Coudert. "No problem," the others answered and on the discussion went. As we left, feeling all questions had been answered, Mr. Coudert once again insisted we not forget the sardines.

It had been agreed to have our picnic on Bastille Day, July 14, France's big holiday. It turned out to be a beautiful, warm, sunny day. At the entrance of our little cul-de-sac, Mr. St. Roch had placed a saw horse with a large notice attached. It read: "The National Assembly has decreed today, July 14, 1977, to be the date of the First National Holiday Picnic of the independent state known henceforth as the *Lotissement Clos Fleuri*," (the name of our development).

The neighbors all brought tables and benches. The picnic was held in the garden of the St. Roch family. All the inhabitants of the street were invited, from two-year-old Eric to Grandmère Trichet. Mr. Coudert was the first to arrive. He wanted to be sure the grill was definitely ready for the—sardines. When I arrived with my contribution, I felt I was getting some rather odd reactions. I placed my salad and dessert on one of the tables and went off to see where I could be of some help. When my back was turned, Mr. Marty cornered Peter to ask what I had brought. He pointed to my salad—a Jello Sunshine salad—and asked: "What is that?" as if it had come from outer space. Peter explained. Then Mr. Marty pointed to my dessert—a two-layer chocolate cake—and whispered: "What is that?" Again, Peter explained. I guess the French are more used to one-layer tortes or several very thin layers. With much teasing and laughter and good food, the picnic progressed—including the sardines.

Mr. St. Roch had been having a battle of wits with an unwelcome mole in his garden. He had set a trap, and early every morning before he went to work, he would rush out to the garden to see if he had caught the mole. Peter and the two Coudert boys thought it would be funny to spring the trap. They took a bite out of the carrot and left a note saying, "Thank you for the carrot" and signed it "Mr. Mole." They rushed over to Mr. St. Roch to tell him the news. Mr. St. Roch really thought he had the mole until he read the note. He spent the rest of the afternoon accusing everyone there of being the culprit, but never once accused the boys, who were convulsed with laughter all afternoon.

In the evening the picnic continued in the St. Roch garage. When a phonograph was found, the revelers did not approve of the music, so a raid was made on our house for American Rock and

Roll. We danced, drank, and ate until 11 PM. But, there was so much food left over, it was decreed that the feast be continued the next day, Sunday.

At 11 AM, the group resumed the celebration. By now everyone was well fed and content. Conversation was much quieter. Mr. Coudert was still grilling sardines, and Mr. St. Roch was still trying to find out who Mr. Mole was. The group cleaned up and left to return home at 5 PM. Each family still carried some food home. As they left, the boys revealed their prank, and joining in the general laughter, Mr. St. Roch agreed the joke was on him.

I think we shall never forget our first neighborhood picnic in France and the beatific smile on Mr. Coudert's face as he patted his stomach, no doubt filled with a year's supply of sardines.

Love from all to all,
Audray

*Audray Noyes, born in Brooklyn, has lived in Metuchen over 40 years. A French major graduating from Hunter College, she put her French to use first as a bilingual secretary for the former transatlantic French Line and later accompanying her family of two children while her husband worked in France. Before her husband retired and even more since, she has traveled extensively throughout the world but is always happy to return to Metuchen.*

# THE NINETEEN EIGHTIES

# GOING HOME

## Muriel Cagney

My dear children, John, Michael, and Bonnie,

    I am sharing the remembrance of my first overnight visit home after marriage to Daddy. Dad and I were married on May 12, 1979. That November, Dad took a course at the Justice Department in Washington, D.C., while working as an assistant U.S. Attorney for the District of New Jersey. I was teaching a class of neurologically impaired children for the South Plainfield School District. Riley School was a half mile from 118 Adeline Avenue, my homestead from third grade till marriage. The only times I did not live there were my college years and the year I taught at Marywood College or, as you like to call it, "Scarywood"!

    You know your mother has never been a particularly brave soul, so it made sense for me to move back to "118" while Dad was in D.C. I was closer to work, and I could sleep in my old twin bed across the room from Aunt Carol. That was the group at "'118": my mom and dad, my sister Carol, and Nanny, my mother's mother. Of course, you three know every one of these people except my mother, since she died in May of 1980, two months after your birth, John. At the time of my temporary re-entry into my family of orientation, I was expecting you, John.

    My mother was especially happy to have me back under her roof. When I arrived home after school the first day of my visit, I remember saying, "I hope this is okay, Mommy?" I was thirty-two years old, and I still called her "Mommy." Most of the time it was okay, except when I'd call out in a department store for her—

"Mommy?!"—she would blush and say I sounded as if I were seven. The reality was we were as close as two imperfect people could be in this imperfect world. Well, I was imperfect; I thought my mother was perfect! This might not sound like the thought process of an educated, enlightened woman of my generation, but it was truly how I felt then and now.

Getting back to my arrival, Mom's misty response to my question was, "Muriel, this is your home; it will always be." I walked through the first floor to the living room. There was Nanny, feet up in her recliner, watching the news on TV. Dad was in his corner of the sofa, reading the evening paper, having his pre-dinner scotch. Carol was out shopping but would be home for dinner. I went up to my old room, unpacked, and looked around. My sister's threat of taking down my bed the day after my wedding had obviously been thwarted by my mother: "It will be an extra guest bed, Carol."

Nothing seemed changed, except me. I was married and expecting our first child.

We ate dinner in the dining room. We always ate there when all five of us were home for dinner. It was a Monday evening, which meant lots of senior citizen conversation. Nanny was the president of the South Plainfield Senior Citizen Club, which met on Mondays. Nanny kept the address list with phone numbers near the kitchen phone. I remember my cousin Jeffrey, who lived across the street and was Nanny's youngest grandchild, asking, "Nanny, what do all those X's mean on your list?" "Oh, they died," she replied. Nanny never sugar-coated anything.

So, here I was back in the dining room, sitting at the table where I had written my wedding invitations not even a year before. This was the same dining room that gathered us for countless Christmas Eve birthday celebrations for Carol, Thanksgiving dinners, green beer on St. Patrick's Day, dinners Carol and I pretended we had cooked for potential suitors, family pow-wows, but mainly nights like tonight. It was just a regular Monday evening in November, already dark outside, roasted chicken with mushroom sauce, the Irish staple baked potatoes, and family small talk:

"You're not eating your potato. Are you on a diet again?" "You're eating too much; you're going to get fat." "Oh no, you're going out with him tonight—another episode of beauty and the beast!" " I don't want to go to Bay Head again this summer; we should try someplace else." "Where?" "I don't know." "Your father loves the shore."

Tonight was different conversationally. We were discussing names for Bill's and my first child. I liked Bridget, Nanny's mother's name, and so did Nanny. "I like double names, especially Mary Margaret," Mommy said. Carol got out the book we had bought in Ireland, *Irish Names for Children*, and started reading aloud, "Abban, Alaois, Mairead . . . ." We howled with laughter. If we couldn't pronounce the name, how could anybody else! We had plenty of time, since the baby wasn't due until the end of March.

Still discussing names for "our new little darling," we started to clear the dishes. That's what Mother called our unborn baby; that's just what she wrote on the tag of the musical teddy bear the next month at Christmas.

Everyone went to bed, but Mommy and I stayed up very late talking. Here I was, the new bride, asking questions of a woman married for thirty-six years. Eventually, our conversation came back to the baby's name. "Muriel, Daddy never had a son. If it's a boy, he could be John Douglas after the two grandfathers. And don't forget your godfather, Uncle Michael, or 'Mickey' as everyone called him." Uncle Michael, the dashing *bon vivant*. I can still see the bluest eyes and biggest smile that went with the spontaneous soft-shoe dance he always went into for me. He was with my father the night I was born.

"Okay, Mommy, but you know the girl's name Bill and I really like is Muriel Bonaventure, which means 'good things to come.' The Muriel would be after you, Muriel the third, but we would call her Bonnie!" Mom said, "I love that—I knew the loveliest girl named Bonnie in high school." Mommy always associated a name with a person.

We talked a lot longer. Instinctively, Mom knew how happy I was being married to Bill, and we were all so excited about the new baby in our family. We kissed good night; she patted me on the back while giving the spontaneous wink she always gave me.

I got under the covers smiling. I never did agree with Tom Wolfe—you *can* go home again. And like Dorothy, I thought, "Home is best."

So you see, my darling children, John, Michael, and Bonnie, although your "Grammy" only held John briefly in her arms, Muriel Grace held each of you in her thoughts and in her heart then and now . . . and she goes together with you like a wink and a smile!

As ever,<br>Your loving Mother

---

*Muriel Scherr Cagney has resided in the Metuchen-Edison area all of her married life, along with her husband Bill and their four children, John, Justin, Michael, and Bonnie. A graduate of Marywood University in Scranton, Pennsylvania, with a Master's Degree in Special Education from the College of New Jersey, she has taught on both the elementary and college levels in her field. Muriel currently divides her time between her giftware business, "Remembrance of You," and volunteer work in church and education activities.*

# TRANSFORMATION

## Jessie Flynn

Dearest Children,

Nineteen years ago, at the age of thirty-six, my life changed dramatically. Having lived a rather conventional existence, I was quite unprepared for what I experienced that summer morning. Indeed, until now, sharing it has been reserved for a mere handful of intimates.

At the time, my husband Dennis lay in a hospital bed in New York recovering from his second brain surgery to correct complications from a cerebral aneurysm. Our three young children played at home under the watchful eye of my mother while I dashed off for an appointment to have my hair cut and then spend a restful day at a retreat House of Prayer. For two weeks I had virtually set up camp at Denny's bedside and thought a break might restore my spirits. Or perhaps it was my husband who insisted I take the day off; he needed space from my nurse-like hovering over him.

By nine-fifteen that morning, hair-shorn but feeling world-weary and none-too-beautiful, I took a brief detour to visit a friend. Robin had been praying for our little family and I wanted to give her an update. Well, the tears started to flow as I poured out my fears about Denny's survival while she knelt at my feet, held my hands, and prayed. I can't even remember the words she said.

Suddenly, I felt an overwhelming exhaustion. Contrary to all social propriety and certainly very late for my date at the House of Prayer, I found myself resting, feet up, legs covered by an afghan, in her living room lounge chair. The strangest thing was that I wasn't asleep. In fact, I heard Robin in the kitchen. I wasn't fully conscious either. Instead, I felt immersed in a twilight zone. Angels, firmly positioned on my outstretched legs, prevented me from getting up. They seemed like genderless beings that I simply knew were angels. At my left shoulder a male figure who I sensed was Jesus held his arms around me and spoke in my ear: "Be still and let me love you." Trust me, I couldn't have moved if I'd wanted to. Words emitted from a painting on the wall; it was as if the painting said, "I am God." Yet I knew that wasn't God. And all the while my entire self felt permeated with such an exquisite love and peace that will never be adequately described. If someone had given me a choice to leave this "place," I would have stayed forever.

Alas, Robin came in and gently announced that she had made some lunch, that I had been sitting there for over three hours. Three hours? Impossible. It seemed like a wink of time, like time had stood still. I inquired about the painting, which she explained was a lighthouse on the rock. Oh my, it was the beacon of light that had been talking. Oh dear, I must keep this precious experience to myself, I thought. It really felt too deep for words.

Later that day friends and family members noted a change in me: an inner quiet, a profound sense of peace, a palpable "lovingness," in the words of Mother, who called me into the library that night. Mystified by my radical transformation, she inquired about what had happened. All I said was that Robin had prayed. "How?" Mother prodded. I replied that it really didn't matter. Indeed, I could've been hanging upside down in a well and it wouldn't have mattered.

I never did get to the House of Prayer. But I witnessed the power of prayer or what I call an openness to the Other. That day I found out that there is a love out there, in us, around us, that is the only thing that matters. It is deeper, simpler, and purer than all the codes and rules and busyness that we clutter our lives with. It is the love that dispels fear and connects us to each other and all things. It is the love that empowered me to become involved in social action, that enables me to help others heal, and that gives integrity behind words of hope about a glorious dimension beyond this material world to those who grieve.

Today Dennis is fine. My mother has died. And twelve years ago our fourth child was born. The sacred circle of life goes on. But my life will be forever changed.

For years I have tried to recreate this experience. With no luck. Others have witnessed moments of light and described them as mystical in their writings. Grace. Mystery. Light. These words now humble me and hold new meaning. But ever since that day, it is love that beckons me. That's THE WORD. Practicing loving kindness is my mission.

YLAD (Your loving and devoted)<br>Mother

*Jessie Flynn, mother of four, is a lecturer, writer, educator, workshop leader, grief consultant, trainer for bereavement caregivers, and volunteer coordinator of social outreach programs. After graduating from Gettysburg College, she continued advanced study at the University of Pennsylvania and Drew University, where she specialized in pastoral counseling.*

# THROUGH THE LOOKING GLASS

## Helen Stapley

Dear Victoria and Rachel,

When your Grandpa Edward went on his business trips to Madrid, Spain, he always said that he was going to go "through the looking-glass" again. I had always thought that it would be so interesting and lots of fun to live in another country for a while, especially if that country could be Spain.

It was not until the year 1988 that the possibility of working and living in Spain began to develop. From the time he had begun to work in Spain, Grandpa Edward, now "Eduardo" while in Espana, made an average of two trips to Espana of about a week or more in duration every year. Also during these years two or three Spanish employees would visit the company in New Jersey. Our family was learning about the country of Spain and was practicing speaking Spanish. Even our black dog Angus learned some Spanish words!

In 1988, Grandpa made a usual trip to Madrid early in December so that he could be home in New Jersey in time for Christmas. While in Madrid, he visited several apartments in which we might live beginning in 1989. With an *amiga,* he was able to settle on a very comfortable and convenient place for us to live.

Before our family of two could officially move into the apartment in Madrid at Raimundo Fernandez Villa Verde 40, there were many preparations to be made. There was much "red tape" involved in obtaining permission to stay in Spain longer than the usual time allowed for tourists. Grandpa needed to get a work permit, and I had to get a residency permit. Getting these permits required many trips to New York City to visit the Spanish Consulate. Filling out endless forms, we sat in their waiting rooms for many hours.

Finally, in January of 1989, we left for JFK Airport with our bags and dressed for winter. Upon arrival at Barajas Airport north of the city, we were met by some of our Spanish friends. It was a great feeling to see familiar faces after passing through the customs inspection and walking through the doors into a sea of Spanish people (of course). Being ushered into a comfortable waiting car with the company driver and taken to our spacious new apartment completed the warm welcome.

We proceeded to get acquainted with the neighborhood and the two U-shaped apartment buildings which faced each other to make a big inside garden and lawn. The first floors of most of the buildings in the city were (and are) occupied by stores, businesses, and restaurants, so shopping was very convenient. We were already familiar with St. George's British Embassy Church from our former visits. Now it was about a fifteen minute drive instead of a walk of a few blocks from our old hotel, the Wellington. Those rides were a pleasure, however, in our lovely silver Opal car, which went with the apartment and the job. On weekends I could drive the car!

There was a coffee hour after the church service, and we actually got to know some of the people at St. George's at those times. In the warm weather, cold drinks, even wine, were served on the patio under the grape arbor. The little parish house had used paperback books for sale, and we bought them at bargain prices. There was an especially good paperback on Spanish cooking. Also, there was a collection of magazines for and about English-speaking people.

It was in an English magazine that an organization called "The American Women's Club" was discovered by me. There were an address and telephone number listed for the club in Madrid. After thinking for several days about what the club might really be, I actually called the number. At least I had learned how to use the telephone! The club secretary gave me some information and directions for finding the club house. How nice that club house was! What good activities there were, and, of course, what interesting and friendly people were there. Many interest groups were offered at the club, including a book discussion group, language studies, trips and walking tours, card games, and crafts. Joan, the leader of the book discussion group, and Shirley, another active member, lived just a few blocks from our Villa Verde apartment.

A typical visit to the AWC clubhouse began by walking out of our apartment house to hail a cab to the Plaza de Ecuador. The club occupied two floors of a building on a short street off the plaza. One needed to ring the bell and give the proper identification to be "buzzed in."

Many of the club members were also members of St. George's Church. Some club members did not speak English as a first language, since membership in the club required only being an American or being married to an American; hence, the name "The American Women's Club." As a result, there were ladies from South America, Europe, and Asia—an interesting mix of women.

Because both Joan and Shirley lived on the Avenida Castellana near our street, sometimes I shared a taxi with them when going to or from the club. Both ladies were Americans; Joan had been a school administrator from Long Island, New York, and Shirley had lived in several United States places, including New York City.

One day, Joan, Shirley, and I had planned to have lunch at one of their favorite restaurants. Before taking a taxi into the "old city," Joan had invited us to *tomar una copa,* literally "to take a cup" in her lovely apartment. The apartment reflected the unique work of Joan's husband. He was a European who did fine work in metal at his atelier, that is, workshop, in the city of Toledo, making swords and armor. He was also a fencing instructor. The large living room had comfortable couches and chairs arranged around a big, low map cabinet which was used as a coffee table.

Joan served us delicious appetizers of the usual Spanish fare: olives, almonds, cheese, and crackers with a wonderful pale yellow dry sherry or *jerez-fino*. After a period of polite conversation, Joan announced that she had some special news about her granddaughter Gail, whose portrait she was showing to us. Gail had become engaged to marry a seminary student in New Jersey. The amazing part of the announcement was that the young man was from our own Metuchen church, St. Luke's Episcopal! We toasted the happy young couple with our sherry. The groom-to-be lived within two blocks of our home in Metuchen!

Although 1989 rushed by very quickly, it was a year filled with wonderful experiences. We made several round trips (*ida y vuelta*) to Spain, had many house guests for travels of adventure in Madrid and other cities, and even made trips to Florida and Ontario (for fish camp, of course).

Back in our home in Metuchen we settled into the routine as though our "through the looking glass" year were just a dream. Later on, a special summer wedding took place at our St. Luke's Church. On that occasion I was able to see again my Madrid friend Joan, the grandmother of the bride.

> Your lucky grandmother says,
> "Adios!" and "Hasta Luego!"
> Grandma

PS As I end this epistle, Grandpa and I are getting out our suitcases for a visit to Madrid and our Spanish friends!

*Helen Stapley was born in South Dakota and lived in Bergen and Middlesex Counties, New Jersey. After graduating from Douglass College, her chief career was raising three daughters. She also worked in statistics and two school systems. Currently, she enjoys being an art museum docent at Rutgers University.*

# THE NINETEEN NINETIES

# NEWPORT, OREGON—1998

## Bernice Bransfield

Dear Rita, Joan, and Carol,

The ocean is a wonderful place to witness the final years of the twentieth century. Even though it is 1998, some things remain constant, just as they were when we were the four McGivney sisters living in Staten Island. Waves still crash on the shore, tides still ebb and flow, and our family continues to grow, change, move apart, and reconnect. Our journey to Oregon this summer reinforced what I had learned—that there are cycles in nature just as there are cycles in life. The secret is to pay attention and listen.

Dan and Jennifer had chosen the rental home in Newport, Oregon, for our family get together. They told us it was lovely—on a cliff above a wide beach, with a perfect view of the Pacific Ocean, where whales swim near the shore.

In order not to be disappointed, I envisioned a rather dingy home in a crowded area with well-used furniture. As we drove up to the home, I felt as if we were entering a dream. The gate to the compound had to be unlocked, and there was parking near the lawn for the caravan of vehicles which were bringing all fourteen of us to this beautiful area for a week's family reunion. Each car was filled with family members and supplies for their favorite activities. The largest vehicle carried Neil and Angie's 22-foot double kayak for paddling on the nearby rivers.

We began to unpack the cords of wood for the fireplace, and the numerous sport bags and ice chests were moved into the proper rooms. Within one hour we all knew where we were going to sleep. Bags were unpacked, and we found the trail from the house on the cliff to the rugged descent through the woods to the grand expanse of sand that was to be our playground for the week.

We were on the Oregon coastline to celebrate our 45$^{th}$ wedding anniversary and all the other special events during the past three years when we could not be together. Our family traveled from Seattle, Washington; Portland, Oregon; Santa Cruz, California; Chicago, Illinois; Branchburg, New Jersey; and Metuchen, New Jersey. It was a monumental feat for all to be available for the same week in August of 1998.

Bill felt younger than his seventy-three years when he was on the isolated beach building a driftwood shelter with his grandsons Ben and Will. The building took all day, and occasionally a stranger would walk by and ask for a tour of the construction. At nightfall the family gathered at the newly built fort on the beach and roasted marshmallows as the sun set over the gentle Pacific.

Will, all of five years old, loved to get into the sand and water. He played with such abandonment. His brown hair would be filled with sand as he grinned with joy at his play. Each time Will came home from the beach, he knew he would take a quick bath and put on dry clothes. In preparation for the warm bath, he would strip at the front door of the secluded home and run directly to the bathroom. My job was to get him in and out of the tub as quickly as possible. With fourteen people and two bathrooms, we were all on a quick time schedule in those rooms.

Feeding the large family could have been a chore, but everyone loves to cook and even loves to do kitchen clean up. The kitchen was equipped with every conceivable appliance and tool, so we cooks had no excuses. Time spent in the kitchen passed quickly because of the view of the Pacific Ocean from the large window over the sink. Dylan, a professional fisherman, cooked mouthwatering marinated salmon on the grill. Instead of cakes to celebrate our gathering, we were presented with Claire's homemade pies.

Shannon was baptized while we visited the West Coast. She is the little joy of our family. We all talked to her with cooing and songs as she responded with her own attempts at speech.

In the evening our family gathered in the large, vaulted living room with a fire crackling in the fireplace. The doors of the porch would remain wide open so that we could all view the moon hovering over the Pacific. On one particular evening, Dan asked a general question, "What is the symbol of the third wedding anniversary?" We all guessed our different answers, and Dan responded negatively. He then brought out an old, decorated, Italian accordion and presented it to his musically gifted wife, Jennifer. He proclaimed, "The accordion is the symbol of the third anniversary! Happy Anniversary, Jennifer!"

Claire held Shannon as Jennifer played the beautiful anniversary gift. Kevin added the harmonica, Sarah the flute, Dan the violin, and Neil the spoons. Our musical family spent the evening entertaining ourselves with songs of celebrations—those from our childhood and those with fond memories.

Possibly everyone felt younger and more carefree that week. There is something about being at the ocean that makes your chronological clock spin backward. Maybe it is the sand that got in all of our shoes, or the sea mist that swirled around us as we walked, ran, and played on the beach. Maybe it was the sheer delight of being with the family we love but seldom see. Whatever it was, for one week we were together as we had been years ago when our family began.

How we wish you could have been with us to celebrate life! You know you were with us in spirit.

          Love,
          Bern

*Bernice McGivney Bransfield graduated from Curtis High School, Staten Island, and earned an R.N. from St. Luke's Hospital in New York City. Wife of William and mother of two daughters and three sons, she has enjoyed reading, gardening, and volunteering for the Friends of the Library for the past twenty years.*

# A NIGHT AT THE OPERA

## Frances Hansen

Dear Johnny,

It was a beautiful late September evening as my son and I threaded our way through the crowds at Lincoln Center. Police were everywhere and the news spread quickly—the President of the United States and his wife were coming to the opera! Bill and Hillary Clinton were coming to hear "Carmen"! The center of the Plaza was kept empty, and people thronged behind the barricades surrounding the sides, hoping for a glimpse of the celebrities. Directly in front of the opera house doors, an area had been cordoned off for the press; cameras were being set up; and reporters were talking into microphones. Up on the roofs of the State Theater and Avery Fisher Hall, security men with rifles were pacing to and fro, an eerie sight against the sunset.

Warren and I passed through the doors of the Met to find ourselves in a line of ticket-holders being searched by government agents equipped with little devices which they passed over the body. When my turn came to be searched, the government agent smiled at me, a smile which quickly vanished when his little device gave a warning signal. Would I step to the side while my bag was searched? Mystified, I stood to one side as they extracted from my bag a little gold box of Godiva chocolates I was saving for intermission. Heaven knows what the Godiva people put into that gold paper (or their chocolates!) but whatever it is, it has enough strength to set off an alarm. Warren chuckled, I blushed, and the government man grinned. Then he handed the box back to me. "I didn't think you looked like an assassin," he said, and passed us on.

Luckily for us, our seats were in a box on the side of the theater, so we had an excellent view of the first balcony center where the Presidential party was to sit. A flag was draped in front of the balcony, and very soon the orchestra struck up the strains of "Hail to the Chief," and down the steps of the balcony came the Clintons, accompanied by Mayor Giuliani and other dignitaries. The audience clapped enthusiastically, the Clintons bowed and waved, and it was several minutes before they could take their seats. Now the chandeliers rose, the orchestra plunged into the overture, and soon we were in Seville. Carmen that night was sung by Denyce Graves, who had been my son's secretary in Boston for a short time, a job she had taken to pay for singing lessons. Gifted with a beautiful sultry voice, she became the definitive Carmen and has played that role all over the world. That night she sang with Placido Domingo, a memorable combination.

During intermission the Clintons graciously stayed in their seats long enough so that the occupants up above and in back of them in the Family Circle could come down to the sides of the theater to stare at them. Both Clintons applauded vigorously at the end of each act; obviously, they were enjoying themselves. After the final curtain they were whisked away magically, and we saw no more of them. I'm sure I'll never be that close to the President of the United States again, and, certainly, it made for a never-to-be-forgotten evening!

Love,
Mom

*Frances Tucker Hansen grew up and married in Metuchen. When her sons reached high school age, she wrote light verse for leading magazines but deserted that in order to construct crossword puzzles for The New York Times and many other publications. She is still constructing and apologizes for the temerity.*

# FAMILY REUNION

## Janet Phillips

Dear Sue,

Before you left, we were talking about families, and I promised I'd write you about our family reunion. This past September all ten of us were able to be together for the first time in two years. (The time before was about five years before that.)

The family who lived next to us in Massachusetts has a beach house which overlooks Buzzards Bay and the Westport River. They have lent it to us in the past and this year was no exception. It's an ideal spot. In the first place, the house has enough room for all of us—which is a big consideration. It is located on top of a small hill, so we could sit on the deck and watch the boats go in and out of the river. A sandy beach is only a two-minute walk away. To make it even better, the nearest houses on all sides are several hundred feet away.

Our youngest son and his girl friend know how I hate to drive, so they flew up from Texas to drive us up and back. They arrived just after our early September storm and spent their first few hours doing much of the heavy cleaning. That was much appreciated, I can assure you.

The next arrivals were our eldest son, his wife and daughter. They flew from Ecuador to Massachusetts the day we arrived. They had to get up at 4 AM and didn't arrive until almost 10 PM—a long day for anyone, especially for their four-year-old. For someone who has four sons, it is a big treat for me to have a visit with a granddaughter . Only being able to see her once a year, if that, is hard.

We had two days with the seven of us before our third son, his wife, and their eleven-year-old son arrived from Connecticut. Unfortunately our second son was very involved trying to sell one house and buy another, so he arrived one day before breakfast and had to leave after dinner that same night. However, even one day with all of us together is precious as far as I am concerned.

What did we do that week? Unfortunately, it was too cold to swim. We all went climbing on the huge rocks at the entrance of the harbor. The Texans went jogging and bike riding. The Ecuadorians played on the beach with their daughter, explored the area, and relaxed—something they don't have time to do at home. The Connecticut gang had such a short time that they spent most of it relaxing, exploring the oceanfront, and visiting with various members of the family. One day a special friend came down and took me out to lunch. We caught up on the lives of our children (ten in all) and had a good "gabfest." My husband and I read, walked, and visited with various members of the family. Of course, all of us took advantage of the opportunity to converse with others alone or in groups, and we had long, talk-filled dinners each night. "Do you remember . . . ?" was a frequent question, and we had many laughs recalling adventures and misadventures from the past.

We always have a clambake one night while we are in New England, since we think nothing can compare to fresh New England lobsters and clams. Naturally, it was the one night we were all together. Our second son is always the cook for this feast. None of the rest of us knows how to do it as well, so it has become a tradition. Aside from that, each family was responsible for one night's dinner—and they were good dinners, especially since I didn't have to plan or cook them! We fixed our own breakfast and lunch. I made sure there was an ample supply of cereal, eggs, cold cuts, cheese, bread, soups, etc., so people ate when, what, and where they wanted.

One of the owner's sons is a close friend of our youngest. He was at our house almost as much as he was at his own when they were growing up. As usual, he came down one afternoon to take the menfolk out for a late afternoon-into-evening fishing trip. He knows all the best spots, so they always catch a lot and have fun doing it. They joked about our gang catching so many fish that they were pulling them in at one end of the boat while he was busy throwing them out the other end when they weren't looking. Of course, we had to feed the fishermen at ten o'clock that night. Needless to say, the rest of us didn't wait for them! The next night this friend and his fiancé came back to cook dinner for us. Freshly caught bluefish and sea bass, done his special way, are a gourmet meal.

The visit came to an end all too soon, but memories last a lifetime. We consider ourselves very fortunate that our children think enough of us and of each other to make the effort—and it was an effort—to have a reunion. We're already thinking about next year. Who knows? Maybe we'll be lucky enough to be able to do it again.

I do hope that your reunion will be as successful as ours was. Be sure to write and tell me about it. Take care!

Love,
Janet

*Janet Phillips was born in a small village in New York State. A graduate of Beaver College, she has been a teacher, counseling secretary and volunteer for various organizations, but, most of all, a wife of 55 years and mother of four sons.*